Praise for
THE PEOPLES' SERMON

"Shauna Hannan is committed to a hospitable pulpit that embraces the lived theological wisdom of the people of God. *The Peoples' Sermon* is a treasure trove of best practices for considering and then engaging in such preaching. Hannan details a process through which collaborative preaching can be explored and modified to fit differing congregations and situations. Along the way, she provides useful ideas and tools for implementation. Elegantly written and gently persuasive, this book is essential reading for preachers who want to embody more genuinely relational forms of preaching and ministry."

—John S. McClure, Charles G. Finney Professor of Preaching and Worship, Vanderbilt Divinity School

"Decades ago, the Scottish theologian P. T. Forsyth said, 'The one great preacher in history is the church.' Now, in this refreshing volume, *The Peoples' Sermon*, Shauna K. Hannan brings this claim to life with a process of sermon preparation that is collaborative, community-based, energizing, and elegantly practical. Hannan provides a way for congregations not only to find their voices in the ministry of preaching but also to be drawn deeper into the mission of Christ. A splendid contribution."

—Thomas G. Long, Bandy Professor Emeritus of Preaching, Candler School of Theology, Emory University

"Shauna K. Hannan makes a convincing case that preaching is a ministry of the whole people of God. Accessibly written, *The Peoples' Sermon* is an excellent guide for anyone venturing into a homiletical journey toward a collaborative ministry of proclamation. Learners of preaching will be equipped to employ a backpack full of hands-on homiletical tools to make a radical shift from solo and solitary preaching to transformative practices of preaching with people."

—HyeRan Kim-Cragg, Timothy Eaton Memorial Church
Professor of Preaching, Emmanuel College,
University of Toronto

"Shauna K. Hannan reminds us how to make preaching whole again by including the whole congregation. Theologically informed, ecclesially grounded, and practically wise, this book calls for the collective stewardship of the pulpit. In a selfie world, this is a timely call to 'we,' rather than 'me,' when preaching. In a divisive society, this book is a challenge to do preaching 'with' rather than 'against' or 'at' others. Readers will come away with a fresh understanding of the contribution the whole body of Christ can make to the ministry of preaching. *The Peoples' Sermon* is an invitation for us all to walk together on the road of gospel proclamation."

—Luke A. Powery, dean of Duke University Chapel and
associate professor of homiletics at Duke Divinity School

"One of the key motifs in postmodern culture is collaboration— people working together to add strength to strength. In this important book, Shauna K. Hannan proposes a collaborative approach in which preacher and congregation work together on sermon preparation, sermon feedback, and other important aspects of preaching. *The Peoples' Sermon* offers a simple but theologically and existentially probing pattern for such work, abbreviated KWHL: What do I *know* about the congregation in relationship to the direction of the sermon? What do I *want* to know? *How* will I find it out? What do I *learn* in the process? The collaborative preacher is no longer the isolated voice in the pulpit but is part of an energizing community of preparation and reflection."

—Ronald J. Allen, Professor of Preaching, and Gospels and Letters (Emeritus), Christian Theological Seminary; coeditor of *Preaching God's Transforming Justice: A Commentary on the Revised Common Lectionary*

"In this wise and energizing book, homiletician Shauna K. Hannan does what she commends. Page by page, Hannan treats her readers as partners and collaborators in uncovering the hidden homiletical treasures of a collaborative approach to the preaching event. Hannan reframes that event so that, far from being a twenty-minute Sunday morning monologue, preaching becomes a Spirit-infused, collaborative practice. Week by week, congregation and preacher together mine that fertile matrix where biblical text, everyday experience, theological insight, and world events interact. And week on week, as one voice begins to proclaim, both preacher and congregation lean in, eager to hear what the Spirit has been saying not simply *to* the church but *through* it."

—Sally A. Brown, Elizabeth M. Engle Professor of Preaching and Worship; director, Joe R. Engle Institute of Preaching, Princeton Theological Seminary

"Preaching should not and need not be a solo performance or spectator sport. It is, rather, a Spirit conversation in which all members of the faith community play a vital role and can have an active voice. Shauna K. Hannan makes an inviting—indeed, compelling—case for congregational collaboration in the preaching act through a vision grounded in Scripture, theology, science (natural and behavioral), and the arts. She fleshes out this vision with a panoply of practical strategies for participatory preaching at every stage—sermon preparation, sermon delivery, and post-sermon reflection. She invites us all into an experiential understanding of preaching as the action and agency of the whole body of Christ."

—David J. Schlafer, preaching consultant; author of *Playing with Fire: Preaching Work as Kindling Art* and *Preaching What We Practice: Proclamation and Moral Discernment*

THE PEOPLES' SERMON

THE PEOPLES'
SERMON

*Preaching as a Ministry
of the Whole Congregation*

SHAUNA K. HANNAN

Fortress Press
Minneapolis

To the seminary students in my preaching courses who embraced this process. You have taught me so much.

To Zoë, who kept me company as I wrote this book during the COVID-19 pandemic.

ὥστε ὁ θάνατος ἐν ἡμῖν ἐνεργεῖται, ἡ δὲ ζωὴ [zōē] ἐν ὑμῖν.
(2 Cor 4:12)

CONTENTS

CONTENTS

PREFACE

Preaching is most faithful when it is collaborative. I was not taught this fundamental conviction. Instead, I learned to set aside fifteen hours a week to engage in deep biblical exegesis and craft a coherent, tidy, and (one hopes) poignant gospel message in order to proclaim it with clarity and enthusiasm so that it connects with hearers and their lives of discipleship. After all, the pastor is the one in the congregation who is seminary educated, has the experience, and is called specifically to this task, right? Yes.

And yet, I've come to believe, a person ordained into word and sacrament ministry or otherwise called to preach is not the sole owner of that privilege. A colleague once reminded me that pastors do not *own* the pulpit; they *steward* it.[1] Carefully guarding an unquestioned power and privilege to preach has worked well for many people, including me. Giving up what has seemed to succeed feels risky, however, since it entails the critical questioning of such privilege and the willingness to lean less on it and more on the work of the Holy Spirit in the midst of the community and even on the community itself.

The difference between bearing the responsibility of stewarding the pulpit and the privilege of "owning" it intensifies in churches that are historically and persistently homogenous.

For example, in my denomination, the Evangelical Lutheran Church in America (ELCA), pulpits have privileged white, male, straight, financially well-off, and educated leaders, while marginalizing the voices of others. For us, the key questions are the following: Is this system of privileging faithful? Is it even sustainable? At whose expense has it seemed to work? Whose voices are not being heard? Whose bodies are not being seen? Which perspectives are given a central place at the expense and marginalization of others? I am grateful that our churches are asking these questions in general, and I recommend we ask them of our preaching practices, in particular.

The goal of this book is to help create vital worshipping communities where all know and live out their roles in the preaching ministry of the congregation and beyond. Both clergy and laity will be empowered and equipped in their roles *before*, *during*, and *after* the sermon is preached. This book will encourage reflection on what preaching is and why the church engages this practice, stimulate conversation about various roles in the preaching ministry of the congregation, and guide readers and their communities through a process that will equip them for fulfilling those active roles. The process will benefit not only preaching but also other ministry practices, such as Bible study, pastoral care, Christian education, and fellowship.

Recommendations for Using This Book

In the collaborative spirit of the book, I recommend you make your way through it with others. So go ahead and find your preaching partners now and invite them into conversation from the very beginning. Of course, I also recommend that you do the exercises as you read. I am inspired by the Latin phrase *solvitur ambulando*, commonly attributed to Augustine, which means "it is solved by walking." In other words, we learn things by getting our whole bodies involved. Experts have taught us the science that explains why we learn by doing. Ask the educators and athletic coaches and musicians around you about their experience with this claim, and then put it into practice for the sake of the gospel. Think of the Shema: "Hear, O Israel: The Lord our God, the Lord is one. Love the Lord your God with all your heart and with all your soul and with all your strength" (Deut 6:4–5 NIV). Note that it does not say we are to love the Lord, our God, with just our minds. No, we are to love the Lord, our God, with our whole beings: our hearts, our souls, our strength. Getting our whole beings involved is an act of worship. Yes, collaborative sermon preparation is an act of worship for the priesthood of all believers.

In recent years, students and workshop attendees have responded to my invitation to "try on for size" more collaboration in their preaching ministries. Even the most steadfast naysayers have discovered eager partners. "I had no idea," some say. Others encounter preaching partners who express eagerness for the next opportunity to participate. Others find new life in their pastoral ministries. Here's one testimony (you'll find others throughout the book):

> The feedforward and feedback processes effectively focused my sermon on the context of [my congregation]. The collaborations also shaped my prayer and pastoral life in the community. This latter benefit was unexpected and may have been the chief reward. I connected with a sixteen-year-old about his fear that he had to work harder to earn God's love. I bonded with a new parishioner who senses no room for his conservative

social views in [our] progressive community, despite his fervent love for Jesus. The sermon was better for the collaboration, but even if it had not been, the gift of walking with these people was immeasurable.

Caveats

This book is not meant to encourage anyone to overthrow their preachers; even the process of getting to more collaborative preaching practices should be collaborative and not authoritarian. While I am recommending that preachers "pass the mic," figuratively and perhaps even literally, I am not advancing a kind of liturgical "open mic" session in worship.[2] Certainly not everyone is required to take their turn "in the pulpit." As you will read, there are other ways to participate in the preaching ministry of a congregation. While most congregation members will not be bound for seminary, this book may indeed lead many more people in our congregations (yes, laypeople!) to become equipped as preachers.

Readers will most certainly need to adjust for their context. Some people or communities may not be ready for the adjustments proposed here. Some may not know they are ready, but something in this book might be just the spark to ignite that unfulfilled urge to be more involved. Others know they are ready. Wherever you find yourself on this spectrum, please feel free to adapt this book's contents as needed. You know your context best.

Hopes

Many books on preaching published in the twentieth century and
early twenty-first century propose a more collaborative approach
to the church's preaching ministry. Even so, it is not happening in
practice. My fervent hope is that this book will not only convince
but equip you and your conversation partners to make a collaborative approach to preaching a regular practice. I hope you experience what was expressed above—that is, sermons that are "better
for the collaboration" and the immeasurable gift of walking with
one another.

Acknowledgments

Writing this book has certainly not been a solo endeavor. I want
to acknowledge the following people for their participation,
encouragement, and assistance:

* I am indebted to those preaching professors and homileticians whose proposals for a more collaborative way of
  preaching have inspired me and so many others.
* Thank you to seminary students in the courses I teach
  and seasoned preachers in the workshops I lead who dare
  to try on for size this "new" collaborative way of preaching. Whether or not you are mentioned by name in this
  book, you have influenced it because you have influenced me. I want to acknowledge those who gave me
  permission to feature their work: James Aalgaard, Mary
  Lou Baumgartner, Kevin Beebe, Jenna Bergeson, Brenda
  Greenwald, Linda Hamill, Ben Hogue, Mark Holmerud,
  Kaari Nieuwlandt, and Hallie Parkins. Thank you.

* Thank you to congregation members who have responded to invitations (mine and others') to participate in your community's preaching ministry. Your voices are crucial to the proclamation of the gospel, both in our sanctuaries and in the world.
* Thank you to Pacific Lutheran Theological Seminary of California Lutheran University (in Berkeley) for granting me a sabbatical for the fall semester of 2020.
* Thank you to editor Beth Gaede of Fortress Press and Working Preacher Books for helping me organize the jumble of ideas in my head. You've made this book clearer. Any lack of clarity that remains is solely my responsibility.
* And thank you, readers, for considering the contents of this book. I'd be honored to hear what impacts your preaching ministry.

Soli Deo Gloria

INTRODUCTION

The proclamation of the gospel is the responsibility of the baptized rather than the privilege of the ordained. Dare I say it is not faithful for a preacher to craft a sermon in isolation, step into "the pulpit" (literally or metaphorically) on Sunday morning, offer a one-sided monologue, and, on Monday, start all over with the process of researching and writing in preparation for the following Sunday. Preaching is not a solo endeavor. It is a communal practice, a ministry of the whole congregation. I hope to equip those who are called to preach to, in turn, equip others to fulfill their baptismal call to proclaim. This book offers the what, why, and how of this process. To start, we might need to shift our understanding of preaching.

To Preach *With*

The phrase "Don't preach *at* me" suggests "preaching" is a four-letter word. As a preaching professor, I'm particularly sensitive to the negative idiomatic use of this word, even though I am fully aware of and admit the potential for pulpit abuse and manipulation. Perhaps this use of the word comes from the unidirectional nature of preaching that has become the norm. Sermons often contain (and in some circumstances are expected to contain) verbal (and maybe even physical) finger wags—"You must . . ."

or "You should . . ." Add to this a tendency to think that the preacher speaks at the behest of the divine—"God told me to tell you . . ."—and there is no room for conversation, much less disagreement. What is said is said. Amen!

Does it have to be this way? No. Slightly varying the language of that caustic phrase "Don't preach *at* me" to a more communal "Do preach *with* me" leads to an invitation for the baptized to collaborate with the called preacher in order to fulfill their call to proclaim the good news of Jesus. This collaboration does not get the pastor-as-preacher off the hook. Instead, they are prompted to hook others into the deep study of Scripture and the awareness of how the biblical story continues to be a living word that shapes, challenges, and maybe even reflects our communities.

A preach-*with*-me preaching process invites presermon engagement that offers fodder to the preacher so that preaching connects with people's lived experiences. When the broader community is part of the sermon preparation process, the sermon has more of a chance to "land." A hook is also formed on the back end of the sermon when the conversation continues. People can get hooked on engaging the preacher and, very importantly, one another regarding matters that were addressed in the sermon. For those of you who regularly step into the pulpit (literally or metaphorically), isn't that what is desired? For those of you who more regularly grace the pews, does this sound exciting to you?

Roger Alling and David Schlafer say this kind of preaching mirrors how God is with us. That preposition is key. In the "sacred stories of our faith tradition, God is described as talking *with*, as listening *to*, as deeply honoring the personalities of the human partners with whom God engages in dialogue."[1]

Consider the following statements that will be explored throughout the book:

* God welcomes human participation in the *missio dei*.
* To be church means to operate mutually—that is, with God and with one another.
* The most dynamic and sustainable ministries are collaborative.

These claims are fundamental to the proposals in this book. To the extent that they are true, even if only aspirationally, the key ministry practice of preaching being the work of only one person misses the mark. If you are inclined to respond at this point with "but we've always done it that way," note that this way is not what has always been taught. Despite the efforts of various scholars and professors who have proposed a more collaborative homiletic since the mid-twentieth century, preaching has unnecessarily continued as the practice of just one person in the community.

Various Collaborative Homiletic Proposals

Nearly thirty years ago, Episcopal priest Barbara Brown Taylor proposed that "preaching is not something an ordained minister does for fifteen minutes on Sundays but what the whole congregation does all week long; it is a way of approaching the world, and of gleaning God's presence there."[2] United Methodist scholars Justo and Catherine González warn against "Lone-Ranger preachers":

> The problem comes when we seem to say that [the preacher's] private Bible study is somehow better or deeper or more meaningful than corporate study—when

we forget that the Bible comes out of a community and is addressed to a community. . . . Rather than encouraging their hearers to delve further into the Bible, [Lone-Ranger preachers] actually are discouraging them. . . . The Bible becomes an esoteric book that only those with specialized education or gifts can possibly be able to understand. It is not a book for the lay Christian, but only for the "professional." This is hardly an attitude that should be encouraged in the church.[3]

This sentiment echoes the warning of Dietrich Ritschl decades earlier (1960), who said, "Part of the cruelty (which we ourselves have created) of our Church is that minister and congregation are separated in such a way the preacher is alone and isolated with [the] preaching task."[4]

Other members of the Academy of Homiletics have pushed toward collaborative preaching (in its many possible forms). Especially notable was the work of two Presbyterian (PCUSA) preaching professors from the United States who wrote homiletical textbooks that emphasized preaching as a collaborative venture. John McClure advocated for collaborative sermon roundtables in order to help the preacher take sermon preparation "out of the pastoral study and into the context of roundtable conversation."[5] Lucy Atkinson Rose proposed a conversational preaching model that is "communal, nonhierarchical, personal, inclusive, scriptural."[6] This nonhierarchical, communal relationship between pastor and congregation questions traditional assumptions of preaching and offers insight from those on the margin and those outside the field of homiletics.

Nearly a decade later (2005), United Methodist O. Wesley Allen Jr. picked up Rose's proposal and wrote *The Homiletic of All Believers: A Conversational Approach to Proclamation and Preaching* in which he outlines a conversational ecclesiology and homiletic.[7] Yet another decade passes before (ELCA) Lutheran David Lose wonders, "If our people have spent their entire lives watching others [preachers] talk about faith but have never themselves had an opportunity to do so, where will they have developed the competence and confidence to do it themselves?"[8] Lose goes a step further than what a fellow Lutheran, Herman Stuempfle, noted decades earlier: preaching's purpose is to equip laypeople for their missionary work in the world.[9]

Patrick W. T. Johnson (PCUSA) follows suit in *The Mission of Preaching: Equipping the Community for Faithful Witness*, about which Lose writes in the foreword: "[Johnson] challenges us to shift our understanding of preaching from a clearly defined practice employed by a single practitioner and the delight, wonder and appreciation of a receptive but largely passive audience to an emerging, but still under construction, practice that seeks to equip both more traditional and seeking Christians alike not only to understand their faith but to share it."[10]

This concept of preaching understood as a ministry of the whole congregation is not new, and the chapters in this book will show this to be even more foundational (biblically, theologically, and ecclesiologically) than has been recognized. Aligning our practices with this understanding of preaching can help avoid homiletical pitfalls such as discounting the interpretive input of a broad set of voices, advancing the "agenda" of one voice, and "burning out" the preacher. Many Christian communities have experienced all three results despite the high hopes we have for preaching. Making the practice of preaching more collaborative and participatory has the potential to

a. increase biblical fluency,
b. include voices that have been left out or disregarded,
c. strengthen sermonic illustrations,
d. give confidence to and increase competence for those who are timid about sharing how God works in their lives,
e. create opportunities for caring for one another, and
f. guide the church in becoming more engaged in the world.

This book will guide preachers and preaching partners alike in articulating what preaching is, why it is a vital ministry, and how to engage it more collaboratively. The first three chapters offer foundational theory. The subsequent four chapters offer ways to put the theory into practice. The chapters proceed as follows.

Outline of Chapters

Chapter 1: "What Is Preaching?"

A goal of chapter 1 is to help you formulate a working definition of preaching. Definitions and expectations greatly impact how one preaches and how others listen to and otherwise participate in sermons. Numerous definitions will be provided in order to prompt reflection and conversation about the various ways people understand preaching. This exploration is useful for speaking both theologically (God's role) and anthropologically (human's role) about preaching. Your "working" definition will provide the foundation for reading through this book and confidently participating in conversation with others about what preaching is and what is desired and expected from preaching.

Chapter 2: "Why Preach?"

Chapter 2 assists in responding to the question "Why preach?" by identifying on what basis we preach. Biblical, theological, rhetorical, historical, and ecclesiological bases will be explored. Doing so will undergird the claim that preaching can be—indeed, is meant to be—a ministry practice that involves a community.

Chapter 3: "The Case for Collaboration"

Chapter 3 ventures into other arenas in life that embrace collaboration, often to broaden and deepen participation. We will explore some examples of collaboration from the natural world as well as consider how collaboration is fundamental to who we are as humans. A brief foray into the ways education, technology, and the arts thrive with collaboration will be instructive. If these arenas recognize the gift and necessity of collaboration, why not the church? Indeed, the church's expressed ecclesiology recognizes the gift and necessity of collaboration. And even some of our ecclesial practices (particularly with regard to mission, evangelism, and biblical studies) model methods of mutuality. With these models in place, we can ask, "So why not preaching? How can this ministry practice thrive with a more collaborative approach?"

Chapter 4: "Feedforward: Collaborative Sermon Preparation"

The next three chapters explicitly move into the "how" of preaching as a ministry of the whole congregation. Chapter 4 helps identify elements of sermon preparation, all of which, as homiletician Tom Long has noted, are not simply preparation for a ministry practice but *are* ministry. And since ministry is generally presumed to be collaborative, preachers will be invited to make their sermon preparation more collaborative. Preachers are encouraged to equip others to participate in that ministry. A feedforward sermon preparation process including practices for congregational and biblical exegesis will be offered.

Chapter 5: "Feed: Stewarding the Pulpit"

While chapter 4 focused on sermon preparation ("before"), this chapter offers possibilities for how the sermon itself might invite broader participation. Sermon excerpts exhibit how collaborative sermon preparation makes a difference in the preaching moment—as one former student called it, "the feed." This chapter exemplifies collaboration by including (1) other preachers' experiences with more participatory sermons that have resulted from their newfound processes and (2) expressions of the difference it has made in their faith communities.

Chapter 6: "Feedback: Beyond Ego Strokes and Ego Strikes"

Chapter 6 suggests ways preaching partners might follow up on what they heard and experienced when the sermon was preached. This opportunity is precisely where Stuempfle's claim that the hearers are propelled into the world to do their missionary work comes into play. "Now what?" is the primary question for this chapter. Questions such as "What was the main point of the sermon?" and "How did you like the sermon?" will be replaced with "According to this sermon, who is God and how does God work in our lives?" and "In what way(s) will this sermon change your thoughts, feelings, and behaviors?"

The concept of "feedback" is less about stroking (or, God forbid, striking) the ego of the preacher and more about helping the preacher understand what listeners actually heard and experienced and the difference that will make in people's lives. A phrase commonly used by preaching professors is apt here: "The sermon isn't simply preaching the gospel; it's getting it heard." The feedback process also continues the process of equipping hearers to gain, as David Lose says, "confidence and competence" to be bearers of good news in their daily lives. Sample feedback forms will be offered.

Chapter 7: "Next Steps: Putting It All Together"

The concluding chapter of the book is the beginning for worshipping communities. Since practices that reflect preaching as a ministry of the whole congregation might be disorienting for preachers and preaching partners alike, a process for how to proceed (including a weekly rhythm) will be outlined. Preachers and preaching partners will be encouraged to amend the proposed "next steps" to suit their contexts.

1

What Is Preaching?

Recall the last time you attended worship as a congregation member. Try to remember the moments right before the sermon, when you were listening to the reading of the gospel, or singing a hymn, or praying, perhaps. As you participated in this liturgical moment and anticipated the sermon, can you identify what you were thinking? What were you feeling? Were you hoping for anything in particular? What were your expectations? A response such as "that depends" to any of these questions makes perfect sense. Indeed, the way we enter into worship depends upon how our week has been, how our children are acting next to us in the pew, how the Scripture readings strike us, and even whether we trust the person who is about to preach. So, yes, it depends. But in general, consider your typical thoughts, feelings, hopes, and/or expectations as the sermon begins. Now anticipating the next time you will hear a sermon, how might you respond to the questions? As the sermon is about to begin . . .

* What will you likely be thinking?
* How will you likely be feeling?
* What might you be hoping for?
* What will you be expecting?

Your responses to these questions begin to clarify your understanding of what preaching is and why you think the church includes this practice in worship. If you noted that you hope to gain an understanding of the Scripture readings that were just read, then you might think preaching aims to teach something about the Bible. If you wrote that you expect to be guided in your life of discipleship in the coming week, then you might think preaching has something to do with morality and ethics—that is, how Christians are to live in this world. If you identified feelings of dread or thoughts that the next ten to twenty minutes will have nothing to do with you and your life, then, of course, you might consider preaching to be irrelevant, boring, annoying, or something to put up with or the part of worship you would like to see eliminated. If you hope that the sermon will comfort you in your grief, then perhaps your faith assures you that the Holy Spirit accompanies you no matter your situation in life. If you hope to be motivated to get involved in addressing the social injustice rampant in your community, then you might acknowledge the power of prophetic proclamation to transform lives, including yours.

Many of us have taken for granted preaching and its place in worship and have never thought to consider these questions. "We've just always done it that way," some might say. This chapter encourages you to reflect on your setting's preaching ministry and your role in it. In doing so, you will be engaging in homiletics—that is, the theological work of reflecting on the art of preaching. By the end of the chapter, you will be able to identify your own understanding of what preaching is and even to assert what you would like preaching to be.

Keeping in mind your responses to the questions above, write your definition of preaching.

Preaching is _____

_____

Let's call what you've written your "working" definition of preaching, since you have the freedom to tweak/amend/upend/rewrite this definition as you read through this book and beyond.

You are in good company in the struggle to write a succinct and clear definition, for many others have attempted to define this multifaceted and adaptable practice we call preaching. Consider this late twelfth-century definition found in the homiletics manual *De Arte Praedicatoria* (*The Art of Preaching*, 1199) written by theologian and homiletician Alan of Lille. Preaching is "the manifest and public instruction in faith and morals, zealously serving the information of [humankind], proceeding by the narrow path of reason and the fountain of authority [Holy Scripture and the writings of the Fathers]."[1] Scholars have acknowledged this as the first formal definition of preaching. What, if anything, in this definition resonates with your experience? How is this definition different from your definition of preaching?

According to Alan of Lille's definition, preaching has a didactic component; it instructs, it teaches. More specifically, it teaches something that has to do with faith and morality (what one believes and how one lives). Preaching is in service of humankind. This definition also recognizes that a twofold authority is at work: the Holy Scriptures and the writings of the early church fathers. Out of this definition, we get answers to questions such as the following:

3

* What is the function of preaching?
* What is the content of preaching?
* To whom is preaching directed?
* Who or what does the practice of preaching serve?
* What authorities are at work in preaching?

Consider how your working definition assists you in responding to any or all of these questions. Don't worry if it doesn't yet, but do notice where it does. Of course, feel free to add to or amend your definition if any of these questions spark something for you.

Preaching is _____

_____

Human's Role in Preaching

Now consider these questions:

* Where in your working definition do you fit into the picture? What is your role?
* Where do others fit into that picture? What is their role?
* How do you and these "others" connect with one another, if at all?

Your responses to these questions help identify the anthropology at work in your understanding of preaching.

The assumed anthropology in some preaching definitions emphasizes the role(s) of the preacher. For example, preaching professor and writer Ronald J. Allen asserts that "the calling of the preacher is to help the congregation move toward a Christian interpretation of the world. The preacher wants to help the congregation learn to think, feel, and act from the perspective of the gospel."[2] Another scholar and writer, Pablo Jiménez, emphasizes the role of the ordained, since his definition integrates many disciplines in a seminary curriculum: "Preaching, then, is an interdisciplinary work where study and interpretation of the Bible meet with systematic theology, the history of the church, Christian education, pastoral care, and speech. Therefore, preaching is an exercise of theological and pastoral integration."[3]

Other definitions highlight the role(s) of the listeners. Recall Barbara Brown Taylor's definition in the introduction above in which she clearly indicates that congregation members play a key role along with the preacher: "Preaching is not something an ordained minister does for fifteen minutes on Sundays but what the whole congregation does all week long."[4] Herman Stuempfle, too, recognizes the effective power at work in the important role of "lay amplifiers scattered in every corner of society." Because "the preacher's voice *by itself* has limited carrying power," it is the listeners of the sermon who, in turn, "incarnate [God's] grace and truth in the whole range of their common life." Stuempfle even claims, "the first business of the individual preacher is to enable the Church to preach."[5]

If your definition has not yet identified the role of the preacher or the hearer, you may want to add something to your definition. These additions could be descriptions of the roles in your current situation or what you have imagined the roles should be. Next, you'll want to consider where God fits into the picture.

God's Role in Preaching

Does God (as Trinity or as one of the three persons—creator or Jesus or the Holy Spirit) have a role in the practice of preaching? If so, how do you explicitly identify that role? Your responses to these questions will help you identify the theology at work in your understanding of preaching. Take, for example, this statement by Mary Donovan Turner: "The purpose of preaching is, as it was for the prophets and as it was for Jesus, to disrupt life so that a space can be created, a space in which the Holy Spirit can work, a space in which the community can rethink, revisit priorities, or receive."[6] Turner acknowledges that the Holy Spirit's active role in preaching is the same as it was in previous eras, when the prophets and Jesus himself preached. First, the Holy Spirit works in life's disrupted spaces. Second, the Holy Spirit and humans are working together in the same space. Indeed, to say that God works through humans is a profound theological statement. Turner's theology of proclamation is clear.

Stuempfle makes a theological claim when he says that "the Word" speaks through the preacher's words and then through the words of the listeners as they move out into the world. "The Word" itself has agency through human communication. Such efficacy is at work in Stuempfle's Lutheran understanding of preaching, that it is nothing less than a means by which God chooses to impart God's grace (i.e., "a means of grace"). That too is a profound theological claim.

Already we have some indication that Christian proclamation is collaborative in various ways—first, between God and God's beloved creation, and, second, among God's beloved children in their various roles.

Shifts in Theories and Practices of Preaching

While there is no one definitive definition of preaching, over time certain emphases have appeared. In fact, the definitions, purposes, and practices of preaching have taken some dramatic turns over the centuries, as outlined by Lucy Atkinson Rose in her book *Sharing the Word: Preaching in the Roundtable Church*. Rose offers a thirty-thousand-foot flyover summary of three main homiletical strands (traditional, kerygmatic, and transformation) and their distinctive characteristics (both theoretically and practically), distinctions that are at times stark and other times subtle. Each strand has aimed to be faithful for its time and still has proponents today.

Traditional Preaching

According to Rose, traditional preaching, with its aim to win consent from the congregation to a truth claim, enjoys the longest-standing commitment. When persuasion is the goal, an emphasis on the use of rhetoric is foundational. *On Christian Doctrine* (Book IV in particular), often considered the first homiletical textbook, is instructive. In it, fourth-century bishop of Hippo, Augustine (354–430 CE), outlines how one might employ classical rhetoric for the purposes of Christian preaching. The dominance of this homiletical voice for numerous centuries is evident in the most common homiletics textbook used well into the twentieth century, John Broadus's *On the Preparation and Delivery of Sermons*. For Broadus, the preacher's main goal is "to tell people what to believe and why they should believe it,"[7] and the purpose of preaching is "teaching and exhorting [the people] out of the Word of God."[8] The direction of communication is one-way, from preacher to listener, with the preacher clearly functioning as the authority and the listeners as the recipients of the preacher's wisdom and expertise. The purposes of traditional preaching are transmission of a central idea and persuasion, and the content includes information about God and propositional truths that are used to persuade. The language employed is considered to be objective and insists on clarity in order to aid transmission of the message.

Compare and contrast this strand of homiletics with your working definition.

∗ Is the aim of preaching in your definition to persuade, to teach about the Bible, or to exhort?
∗ Is the preacher considered the expert or authority figure?
∗ Are the listeners viewed as recipients whose role is to either agree or disagree with the truths offered by the preacher?

If you've answered yes to any of these questions, then perhaps your understanding of preaching aligns with this traditional strand.

The homiletical theory that Rose identifies as "the traditional voice" was modified by proponents of a kerygmatic theory of preaching who promoted sermons that communicate the unchanging heart of the gospel—that is, the *kerygma*.

Kerygmatic Preaching

Rather than the use of rhetoric serving as the foundation for this strand, as it does in some "traditional" preaching, the eventfulness of the word of God is primary. God's word is "an active presence in preaching," and the sermon is an "event in which God speaks a saving word."[9] The work of New Testament scholar C. H. Dodd and theologian Karl Barth is fundamental for this voice in preaching, which emerged in the 1960s and is reflected in others' claims about preaching, including those of Robert H. Mounce: "When the preacher mounts the pulpit steps he [*sic*] does so under obligation to mediate the presence of the Almighty God. . . . He must allow *God* to speak. His words must bear the Divine Word. His voice must be God's voice. He stands before a group of people whose one great need is to be ushered into the presence of God."[10]

The understanding of *kerygma* as both message and event leads to a shift from an anthropocentric emphasis to a more robust theological emphasis. And yet, as "God's mouthpiece," the preacher is still central, which leads some to cite the danger of "mistaking [the preacher's] voice for God's voice."[11] Instead, the preacher's task, notes Norman Pittenger, is "finding new, metaphorical words for the old, unchanging gospel."[12] From there, God will assume responsibility for the efficaciousness of God's word.

Compare and contrast this strand of homiletics with your working definition.

* Is the aim of preaching in your definition to proclaim the essence of the gospel?
* Is the preacher a vessel through which God speaks to God's people?
* Are the listeners the objects of God's salvific word?

If you've answered yes to any of these questions, then perhaps your understanding of preaching aligns with this kerygmatic strand.

Before moving to Rose's third voice in homiletical theory, it is important to address what is meant by the term *gospel*. It is common, perfectly acceptable, and even a good idea to use this term when defining one's understanding of preaching. What is not helpful is to assume that everyone has the same understanding of what is meant by *gospel*.

Some iteration of the following dialogue occurs at some point in nearly every preaching class I teach.

"What exactly is 'the gospel'?," I ask.

"You know . . . the gospel."

"Without using the term *gospel*, tell us what it is," I nudge.

"The gospel is good news."

"Good. Yes. *Euangelion*. Good news. But what kind of good news? Is the news good like winning the lottery or receiving a clean bill of health from your annual checkup with a physician?"

"The good news of Jesus." Now we're getting somewhere.

"And what is the good news of Jesus?"

You get the idea. To steer you from the pitfall of assuming what is meant by "gospel," fill in the blank:

The gospel is _____

or

The good news of Jesus is _____

Consider adding what you've written above to your working definition of preaching.

Those in the kerygmatic tradition might assume that the gospel is one thing for all people and for all time. Rose identifies a concern with the "unchanging" heart of the gospel and highlights others who have voiced concerns. Alvin J. Porteous, for example, warns against a formulation of the gospel that might be "ideologically skewed" because it represents the perspective of the privileged church and ignores the socially and economically liberating dimensions of the gospel.[13] Rose also points to the work of Justo González and Catherine González who say that the interpretation of the Christian faith by the powerful "became normative and was passed on as authoritative, not only to later generations of the powerful, but also to the powerless, who were left with the alternative of either acquiescing to exploitation or rejecting Christianity."[14] Consequently, the church is "faced with the difficult task of disentangling the message of the gospel from these ideological accretions and distortions."[15]

So how does the church engage in such disentangling? González and González, among many other liberation theologians, insist that "the gospel is best understood by those who are powerless and oppressed."[16] Take, for example, the parable of the laborers in the vineyard (Matt 20:1–16). I encourage you to read the parable and then answer this question: What is the good news in this parable?

The good news in the parable of the laborers in the vineyard is . . .

Imagine an actual Christian community in which one might preach.[17] What would be the good news of this parable if preached in

* a congregation in a Detroit suburb in which the majority of people come from the families of auto industry executives,
* a women's prison,
* a small nondenominational congregation in the Rio Grande Valley in Southern Texas, or
* a village in the Guatemalan highlands?

The good news in an allegorical approach (a common interpretive lens for parables) might be this: no matter when people (early in life or in the later years) "accept Jesus as their Lord and Savior," they will be accepted into God's eternal kingdom. In this reading, the ethical implications of the gospel seem to be "postponed" for the "other world."[18]

Pablo Jiménez proposes a possible "Hispanic hermeneutical" reading of the parable. In doing so, the story "reads from the perspective of the 'desempleados,' the unemployed Latinos who stand at intersections of busy streets, waiting for somebody to pass by and offer them twenty dollars in exchange for doing house or yard chores."[19]

> It is not easy to preach this parable at the Aposento Alto because its members *are* the contemporary "obreros" of the vineyard. Their social location is so close to the social location of the text that they have a natural connection to the biblical story. The main topic of the sermon would be God's love for the poor. The sermon would stress God's love for all Hispanics—particularly for those who can be seen in cities like Austin and Los Angeles waiting by the street to be hired. It would also describe the clash between the values of human sociopolitical systems and the values of God's reign.[20]

For Jiménez, the hopeful proclamation of the gospel in this setting would be "God's merciful acceptance of the excluded and the poor." He suggests the following sermon title: "The Survival of the Weakest."

Jiménez's article highlights other interpretations using the "Hispanic hermeneutic." He refers to a commentary intended for Hispanic congregations written by Justo González, who suggests that "the parable contradicts our contemporary labor practices, given that in our culture most people are paid by the hour." The "apparent injustice" is really a "higher justice: the justice of God": "Those who were hired late in the evening were not lazy, they just could not find employment for the day. In hiring them at such a late hour, the owner of the vineyard shows 'interhuman' justice and mercy. 'Interhuman' because it is directed to other human beings, contrary to the traditional understanding of a 'righteousness' directed to God mainly in cultic settings. The workers who came in late will now have enough money to buy food for their families."[21] The good news is that people who earlier could not find work will find work and, thus, be able to feed their families.

Second, José D. Rodriguez interprets the parable as "an exposition of God's grace." Alongside Rodriguez's Lutheran emphasis on the doctrine of "justification by faith through grace" is a "sociopolitical reading that recognizes the ethical demands of the text." Jiménez astutely points out that Rodriguez's "understanding of justification by faith is comprehensive enough to include interhuman justice." Rodriguez recommends renaming the parable "The Parable of the Affirmative Action Employer."

This one example exhibits that while we all might "claim to preach the crucified Christ, the meaning of that proclamation is the subject of considerable difference of interpretation."[22] Claude Thompson suggests the "kerygma demands constant reinterpretation not only by preachers and theologians, but also by 'Christians.'"[23] Said in another way, "Given this redescription of the kerygma, a part of the work of preaching as a communal, ecclesial activity becomes formulating and reformulating the kerygma's provisional content; that is, discerning those dimensions of the Word that become correctives for the future as the distortions of the past and present come into focus."[24]

An unchanging kerygma may not exist, for what is good news to one person may not necessarily be good news to a neighbor.[25] Also, what is considered to be good news to you today may not have been good news a year ago. The notion of "the peoples' sermon" begins to emerge. Minimally, preachers might consider asking a variety of people, "What is the gospel, the good news, in this particular pericope, for you?" (Of course, encouraging them to say more about their response can be particularly illustrative.) Also emerging is attention to the impact of a biblical story on many as opposed to relying on the intent of one. This attention to impact is foundation for "transformational preaching."

Transformational Preaching

Rose highlights another important homiletical strand that represents a shift from "traditional" and "kerygmatic" preaching. The transformational homiletical voices "convey the commonly held belief that a sermon should be an experience that transforms the worshipers."[26] Every sermon seeks to facilitate an experience, whether that be an encounter with Christ, a new kind of seeing, or new ways of being and acting in the world, for example. These sermons embrace more poetic, imaginative, creative, and narrative content. Rather than talking *about* the gospel, the sermon does the gospel to the hearer (à la Gerhard Forde). For example, rather than talking *about* forgiveness, the worshippers are forgiven.

Fred Craddock's book *As One without Authority* jumpstarted this movement in 1974 by critiquing the traditional distance between preacher and listener, promoting "democracy," "dialogue," "listening by the speaker," and "contributing by the hearer."[27] The preacher, therefore, stands "*with* the people, as one of them, under the Word."[28] The "turn to the hearer" era, as it is called, is in full swing with its new emphasis on the sermon's effect upon the listener. The focus has shifted from intent to impact. The congregation members "are invited to participate more substantially in the sermonic event"[29] beyond simply accepting or rejecting the sermon's content; they are led to their own conclusions about their lives. In other words, they participate by finishing their own stories.

Craddock was inspired by Gerhard Ebeling's work on the relationship between the word of God and language and Ernst Fuchs's work on parable interpretation. Both German theologians emphasized the power of language to do things, to change people. Because their theories of language were known as the New Hermeneutic, the theory of preaching Craddock brought to the United States from Germany became known as New Homiletic. This New Homiletic shifts the emphasis from epistemology to hermeneutics—that is, "from certain theological knowledge extracted from the Bible to the interpretation of meaning in particular biblical texts."[30] Sermons that emerge from the interpretive process are understood to be performative; they have an effect on the listeners. Essentially, sermons create experiences that aim to transform listeners.

Compare and contrast this strand of homiletics with your working definition.

* Is the aim of preaching to create an experience or a transformational event for the congregation?
* Is the preacher the one whose words are crafted to create such a transformational experience?
* Are the listeners invited to "complete the story" for their own lives?

If you've answered "yes" to any of these questions, then perhaps your understanding of preaching aligns with this transformational strand.

Rose summarizes the distinctions among the various homiletical voices: "What distinguishes kerygmatic theory from traditional theory is largely a matter of new convictions about the purpose and content of preaching. What distinguishes transformational views of preaching from kerygmatic theory is largely a matter of new conviction about language and form."[31] What distinguishes each of these theories from Rose's proposal for preaching that is more communal and conversational relates to the gap between pulpit and pew—between preacher and congregation.

Conversational Preaching

Rose desires to close the gap between preacher and congregation and promote mutuality, connection, and solidarity.[32] Since Rose seeks a partnership between preacher and congregation, she proposes a conversational preaching model that is communal, nonhierarchical, personal, inclusive, and scriptural and sermons that are offered as proposals that invite counterproposals. The aim of preaching is to "gather worshipers regularly around the Word, to set texts and interpretations loose in the midst of the community, so that the essential conversations of God's people are nurtured."[33] With this approach, "the preacher and the congregation stand together as explorers, while a text, meaning, or mystery lies on the other side or confronts us as Other."[34] Rose takes as her starting point the work of Robert Browne, whose image of preaching is a nurturing process:[35] "In conversational preaching, this sermonic conversation is grounded in solidarity—a shared identity as the believing people of God, a shared priesthood before God and within community, and shared tasks of discerning and proclaiming God's Word."[36] The shift, Rose notes, "is from the preacher's responsibility for upbuilding the church by providing answers or truths to the community's responsibility for its own formation and reformation."[37]

Compare and contrast this strand of homiletics with your working definition by asking the following:

* Do you seek a preaching ministry that is collaborative, shared conversation?
* Are preacher and congregation members partners in ministry, even when it comes to the congregation's preaching ministry?
* Does your definition of preaching encourage equal partners interpreting the Bible together?

If you've answered "yes" to any of these questions, then perhaps your understanding of preaching aligns with this conversation strand of preaching.

Wherever your definition stands at this point, it is important to recognize that one's understanding of preaching shapes how it is practiced.

The "What" Shapes the "How"

Each of these strands—the traditional, kerygmatic, transformational, and conversational—has something to offer, and remnants of each find their way into preaching practices in the twenty-first century. It is time to ask if our definitions of preaching, with their explicit or implicit anthropology, theology, expectations, desired outcomes, and so forth are attainable through our current preaching practices.

Because the "what" of preaching shapes the "how" (at least has the opportunity to do so), take a moment and ask what process—the "how"—will lead to the "what" of preaching as you've defined it. In other words, how will your definition be fulfilled? Let's say, for example, your working definition of preaching identifies a collaborative process involving the priesthood of all believers in order to explore how the biblical story is the living and transformative word of God for our lives "here and now." What practices might need to be implemented in your setting for the preaching ministry to meet this definition?

Another way to explore the relationship between the "what" and the "how" is to explore the current preaching practices (the "how") and consider whether they resonate with the "what" identified in your definition. For example, if the preaching in your context is primarily a kind of lecture aimed at persuading hearers that they should accept the presented truth claims, but your working definition identifies preaching as a means of grace through which God transforms the lives of God's beloved, then there is likely a disconnect in need of attention.

Given the subtitle of this book, it should not be a surprise that I think preaching is a ministry that belongs to the whole congregation. I too have had to adjust my preaching practice to align with this understanding, since I've tended to preach out of the transformational strand of preaching in which the preacher is still the one responsible for facilitating the transformation. Indeed, whenever I preach, I hope that something will happen . . . to all of us. What that something is depends upon a number of factors: the chosen biblical pericope, the occasion, events happening in the world, who the listeners are, my own emotional state. In general, when asked, "What is preaching?" I incorporate the following statements:

* Preaching is a means of God's grace through which we are forgiven, liberated, and healed.
* Preaching helps people recognize that, in Jesus, they are a new creation, freed from having to prove themselves to God and freed for serving the world God so loves.

✳ Preaching instills in its participants (preachers and preaching partners alike) a deep desire to continue to develop a relationship with the living God.

I take as my guide Jesus's sermon as recorded in Luke 4, a sermon that adopts the words of the prophet Isaiah.

The Spirit of the Lord is on me,
    because he has anointed me
    to proclaim good news to the poor.
He has sent me to proclaim freedom for the prisoners
    and recovery of sight for the blind,
to set the oppressed free,
    to proclaim the year of the Lord's favor.[38]

Imagine that. Preaching is a practice that . . .

✳ proclaims freedom for the prisoners.
✳ proclaims recovery of sight to the blind.
✳ sets the oppressed free.
✳ proclaims the year of the Lord's favor.

The word of God is alive and well and fulfills its mission "in [our] hearing" (Luke 4:21).

So the "what" of preaching is connected to the "how" of preaching. Both the "what" and the "how" are connected to the "why" of preaching, the purpose of preaching. Why do we preach? To set the oppressed free, for example. In the next chapter, I explore another way to respond to the "why" of preaching: "On what basis do we preach?"

Before moving to that question, revisit your working definition one more time and use it as a foundation for a group discussion.

Preaching is _____

_____

For Reflection and Discussion

1. Using your working definition of preaching as a starting point, how would you describe preaching to someone who does not attend church?
2. Describe the preaching ministry of your congregation. Be sure to identify your role in that ministry.
3. Do your answers to the first two prompts align? If so, how? If not, what changes can you make to bring them more into alignment?

2

Why Preach?

On what basis do we engage in this communal oral/aural event we call preaching as we do, given that there are so many ways to communicate? Why not email parishioners a reference to the week's biblical story and a few talking points to guide families in their dinner conversations? Why don't we just tweet the summary of our sermon and ask that individuals and families consider how this message might be carried into their weeks? In this plugged-in era of instant gratification, why don't we skip the prompt for reflection altogether and just post a quick interpretation of the pericope on Facebook? Perhaps people have already begun to request these things. And really, it is not too far-fetched to expect that one day a parishioner might come to you with a signature-filled petition to excise preaching from Sunday morning worship. Will you be ready? What will be your response?

Chapter 1 focused on identifying a definition of preaching. In one sense, this definition answers the question "Why preach?" by exploring the purpose of preaching. Another way to respond to the question "Why preach?" is to answer the question "On what basis do we preach?" The difference is subtle but important, since the latter acknowledges the authorities (explicit and implicit) that undergird our practices. Consider this simplified scenario about a child who cleans her room. Why does she clean her room? Perhaps in order to find the lost piece of her favorite puzzle or to receive her allowance. These responses identify the purpose or end goal of her actions. But the child might also answer, "Because my mom told me to clean my room." That response points to the authority that compels her actions. The motivations of the two ways to respond to the question "Why preach?" are distinct; both shape our preaching practices.

So, again, on what basis does your community engage in this communal oral/aural event we call preaching, given that there are so many ways to communicate? Spontaneous responses might include "Because the Bible says we should." Or "God calls us to proclaim." Or "It's the tradition in my church." Because these are common responses, this chapter focuses on the biblical, theological, and ecclesiological bases for preaching. While not exhaustive and not intended to offer the "right answer," this chapter is meant to help you articulate on what basis your community engages in the practice of preaching as it does. Of course, my hope is that doing so will open up the possibility that you will recognize the faithfulness of "the peoples' sermon."

The Biblical Basis for Preaching

"The Bible tells me so." You've heard it. You've said it. You've sung it. What does the Bible say about preaching? Where in the Bible does it say that about fifteen to twenty minutes into a one-hour worship service, one person will step into a pulpit and speak for ten to twenty minutes on a particular section of Scripture (sometimes referred to as the *pericope*, pronounced pə-ˈri-kə-pē) while everyone else sits quietly in order to listen attentively? While putting the question that way might be too flippant, it is important to point out that our practices might not be as sacrosanct as we make them out to be. Still, it is likely true that something in Scripture shapes our preaching practices.

List three or four sections in the Bible that guide your preaching practices. (By all means, feel free to coordinate your responses with others.)

1. _____
2. _____
3. _____
4. _____

Preaching Events

What follows are examples of sections in the Bible that (1) appear to present examples of preaching being practiced, (2) use words that have been translated as "preaching" or one of its synonyms, and (3) feature an experience that is similar to a hoped-for experience in preaching, an encounter with Jesus.

The Apostles' Preaching

A good place to begin is with the Acts of the Apostles, since this biblical book presents a picture of the early church and its efforts for "the Christian message to become understandable in languages and categories people can grasp," as New Testament scholar Matthew Skinner notes. Skinner continues, "Acts does not present the gospel in a one-size-fits-all manner. Every destination [of the apostles] has its particular culture, and bearing witness to God's salvation both attracts and disturbs people in light of those cultural realities. Repeatedly we see how disruptive the gospel can be: it may change how people think about God and the meaning of life, but it also alters core beliefs and practices connected to people's cultural and personal identities, their economic life, their political loyalties, their inherited wisdom, and their hopes for the future."[1] In other words, the power of the proclaimed word of God to transform is evident in *Acts*. Even more, the proclaimed word of God is malleable, according to its context.

I encourage you to take a break from reading this chapter in order to read Acts 2. As you read, identify who is involved, what is happening, and what seems distinctive about the occasion.

Who is involved and in what ways?	What is happening?	What is distinctive?

Already in Acts 2, Peter appears to be preaching. On this day of Pentecost in Jerusalem, Peter stands up in the midst of the crowd to interpret the cacophony of unintelligible speaking from the "divided tongues." Peter takes the immediate context as his starting point, something contemporary preachers are encouraged to do. Peter then refers to Scripture (also something contemporary preachers do). Here Peter refers to the prophet Joel (vv. 17–21) as an authority. He also refers to the Psalms, first to Psalm 16 (vv. 25–28) and then to Psalm 110 (v. 31).

Peter makes some clear theological claims. He reminds those gathered of the power of God demonstrated through Jesus's death and resurrection (v. 32). As he does so, he makes an explicit connection between that power and the experience of the hearers by speaking directly to them: "He . . . has poured out what you now see and hear" (v. 33 NIV). Notice also references to the senses; the whole person is addressed. The climax—an attestation to the Messiahship of the crucified one, Jesus—occurs at what seems to be the end of Peter's preaching (v. 36). Peter is bearing witness; he is testifying (a form of preaching).

Notice what happens to the hearers as Peter preaches, how they are affected physiologically: the message pierces their hearts (v. 37). What do they do next? They don't just walk away grumbling or focused on the next item on their to-do list. They talk with the other apostles and with the preacher himself. They wonder together what they should do.

Peter's response to their reaction is more exhortation: Repent! Be baptized! Receive the gift of the Holy Spirit! It appears Peter is still preaching: "For the promise is for you, for your children, and for all who are far away, everyone whom the Lord our God calls to him" (v. 39). Notice the second-person address again—that is, "doing the gospel": The promise is *for you* (plural!). The promise is fulfilled in the hearing of those gathered, and it is for all others "whom the Lord our God calls to him." One wonders if in the sections written after verse 36 we find Peter still preaching. Or are they engaged in the "after worship" conversation? It seems like Peter is still preaching: he testifies, he proposes arguments, he continues to exhort (vv. 38–40). Did the assembly interrupt in the middle of Peter's sermon? Or, was Peter finished with the sermon and their postsermon questions prompted him to say more than he had planned to say?

Either way, the assembly seems to have a participatory role in the sermon.

Look what happens as a result of preaching: Peter's listeners' lives are changed. Three thousand people are baptized, and their lives of discipleship are filled with teaching, fellowship, and prayer (vv. 41–42). Not every preaching event noted in Scripture yields such fruitful results. Even Peter doesn't always get such a response. Peter's speech, as recorded in Acts 4, despite (because of?) his being "filled with the Holy Spirit" (v. 8), gets a response only from the religious authorities—it gets him arrested (vv. 1–3). Later, Stephen faces even more dire consequences: his speech results in his death by stoning. (See Acts 7.)

Also in the biblical book of Acts is a peek into a number of the apostle Paul's preaching opportunities. After what sounds like a whirlwind tour throughout Asia Minor (during his first missionary journey), Paul and Barnabas sit in the synagogue in Antioch in Pisidia on the Sabbath day (Acts 13:14–52). Someone reads from the law and prophets. And then, perhaps less typically, comes the impromptu invitation from the synagogue official for Paul to exhort the assembly. (The Greek word translated "exhort" is *paraklesis* and can also mean "to offer encouragement or comfort.") In other words, the "special guests" are invited to preach. What does Paul do in this sermon that might serve as guidance for our preaching? Interspersed in the recounting of all that God had done in the past are the occasional interjections spoken directly to the gathered community. For example, "My brothers, you descendants of Abraham's family, and others who fear God, to [you] the message of this salvation has been sent" (v. 26). Paul's second-person proclamation explicitly tells the hearers how the whole story connects to them and why it matters for them. A little further along is another interjection in the present tense: "And we bring you the good news that what God promised to our ancestors he has fulfilled for us, their children, by raising Jesus" (vv. 32–33). Paul moves seamlessly back and forth between the story of Jesus and what this means for those who are gathered. That sounds like preaching, doesn't it? Paul then employs the Psalms as an authority to bolster his words.

Lo and behold, Paul and Barnabas are invited back. They accept the offer. What they discover on the next sabbath is that word has spread, for this time almost the whole city has gathered to hear, as it says, not Paul and Barnabas but "the word of the Lord" (v. 44). The result of this preaching event is different. The naysayers, fueled by their jealousy, challenge Paul and Barnabas. But Paul and Barnabas do not back down. Instead, they call on another authority, this time the Lord himself.

We start to see the cumulative effect of Paul's preaching. After the second sabbath proclamation, some are dismayed, to say the least, and others delighted, an understatement. Indeed, sometimes preaching creates division and may even lead to persecution. Threats prompt Paul and Barnabas to leave, shaking the dust off their feet. Then we get some insight into how they feel about what has just happened. Just when we might think they would feel disappointed, we discover "the disciples were filled with joy and with the Holy Spirit" (v. 52). Later in Acts, we encounter Paul on his second missionary journey.

Again, I encourage you to stop here, read Acts 17, and consider the same questions. (Feel free to do the same as each new story is introduced below. As always, I encourage you to collaborate with others. Perhaps you might make this a "Preaching in Acts" congregational Bible study.)

Who is involved and in what ways?	What is happening?	What is distinctive?

Acts 17 offers two preaching occasions for our consideration. Verses 1–9 tell the story of Paul preaching in Thessalonica as he is accompanied by companions, including Silas. Paul is in the synagogue on the sabbath days; nothing unusual there. We discover Paul "arguing" (or, "reasoning") from the Scriptures (v. 2). (The word for arguing or reasoning is *dialexato* and is related to conversing and even preaching.) Paul is explaining, proving, and setting forth evidence that it was necessary for Jesus to die and be raised again. All of these things are possible models for preaching or moves within a sermon and seem to align with classical rhetorical elements, much like the traditional style of preaching noted in the previous chapter. The word Paul uses to describe what he is doing, the word translated as "preaching" or "proclaiming," is *katangelio*, which shares the root for *eungelion* (the gospel).

Paul's preaching in the synagogue this time yields mixed results, which is not surprising, since these preachers are challenging others' authority (the emperor's, to be precise). In the words of the protectors of such authority, "these people who have been turning the world upside down have come here also" (v. 6). Paul's debate team skill riles up the powers that be. It is worth considering whether or not this story offers a model for preaching.

Moving further along in Acts 17 (vv. 16–34), we read the story of Paul preaching to the Greeks in Athens at the Areopagus (also known as Mars Hill). We have a new situation here, since Paul does not seem to go willingly to the high courts (the Areopagus) but was "brought" there (v. 19). Paul is no longer preaching in the synagogue but in the public square, a very public place indeed. While Paul's debaters brought him to this public place in order to question him, Paul seems to harness it as an occasion to preach. He begins his account by saying, essentially, that he has done his homework; Paul has been exegeting the context, reading the situation, paying very close attention to how these people live, what they know, what they believe, and the like. He speaks his hearers' educated language and appropriates phrases from their authorities (one of their Greek poets, v. 28) to make his point. He even seems to have practiced their "accents," their turns of phrases. In other words, Paul meets the people where they are as he tells them about the God who is truly worthy to be worshipped.

Paul begins his speech (sermon?) by affirming their religious commitments. What seems like flattery, ironically, makes his challengers realize that their seeming religious commitments are misguided. At this point, Paul transitions to direct speech and tells them they too are offspring of this divine one (v. 29). What follows is the pinnacle proclamation: "While God has overlooked the times of human ignorance, now he commands all people everywhere to repent" (v. 30).

As always in preaching, the effect is key. Paul's listeners certainly respond; their scoffing precipitates Paul's departure, though not before some people convert. This time the converts include a woman, which is not insignificant.

Now that we've explored some biblical models in the apostles' preaching, consider whether anything in Acts resonates

*with how you experience preaching in your context. Pick a
recent preaching occasion in your congregation and respond
to the same questions.*

Who is involved and in what ways?	What is happening?	What is distinctive?

You might also ask, specifically, who speaks? Who does not
speak? What do others do while someone is speaking? Is there
any dialogue? What happens as a result of preaching?

Would you say that your setting practices preaching ministry on the basis of any of these biblical stories? In other words,
if someone approaches the preachers and preaching partners in
your context (you, perhaps) and asks that preaching be excised
from worship, would you turn to any of these stories as your
authority—to help them understand existing preaching practices? Might you say, "We preach this way, because Paul did and
it worked. It's in the Bible"?

Jesus's Preaching

One might also say, "We preach because Jesus told his disciples to
do so." But perhaps Jesus himself provides the model of preaching that has led to the way we preach. How *does* Jesus preach? In
parables, for one, of course. Is this a model for our preaching?
Some have tried to write parables, "How hard can it be to talk
about farming and healing miracles and . . . ?" But a story is
different from a parable, right? Our contemporary poets, play-
wrights, screenwriters, and rappers—those who know how to use

words to describe the "stuff" of daily life in a way that builds the tension toward a transformational climax—may have something to teach us preachers, should we want to model our preaching after Jesus's parables. The question remains open, though. Because Jesus preaches in parables may not necessarily mean we should, especially since Jesus indicates, at one point, that he preaches in parables so that they do not understand (see Mark 4:11–12). Of course, using parables is not the only way Jesus preaches.

As is true for Peter and Paul, Jesus preaches in the Jewish worship setting: instruction and explanation follow the reading of the Torah in the synagogue on the sabbath. Traditional preaching, as described in the previous chapter, certainly does model this kind of preaching. But preaching changes once Jesus enters the scene. Not only might Jesus be a model for preaching, but he is also the object of our preaching. That is, in addition to perhaps preaching like Jesus did, we preach Jesus (1 Cor 1:23)!

Luke 4 is a helpful guide here. Jesus is in his hometown and people seem skeptical. You can just hear their tone: "Isn't this Joseph's son?" Jesus opens the scrolls, reads from Isaiah (61:1–2), sits down, then begins to preach. Once again, Scripture prompts us to pay attention to the congregation and not just the preacher. We discover that their eyes are fastened on him. Their eagerness is palpable. Jesus says, simply but profoundly, "Today this scripture is fulfilled in your hearing" (Luke 4:21 NIV). Since the passage indicates this was the beginning of his speaking, it seems likely he would say more. If not, this is the shortest sermon known to humankind, I suspect. And why not, since what we have here are the words of prophets of old being fulfilled by Jesus's presence and in the hearing (!) of his speech.

The gathered people respond, "All spoke well of him and were amazed at the gracious words that came from his lips" (v. 22 NIV). The Greek word translated "spoke well of him" is *emartyroun* and means "to bear witness, offer their testimony." Could we say "the people preached"? In any case, the listeners have a role beyond hearing—that is, to respond: "All were bearing witness to him and marveling at the words." It is unclear if this back-and-forth is to be considered part of the sermon. It seems possible, since Jesus continues (suggesting it wasn't such a short sermon after all). Or, is what comes next a part of the postsermon conversation? In any case, something riles up those who are gathered to the point that they want to kill Jesus. Wow, do words ever have the capacity to affect people strongly . . . and suddenly.

What seems clear here is that, again, with Jesus, something new is happening. Not only might Jesus be a model for preaching, but he is also the object of our preaching. Even more, this section resonates with Luther's claim about Jesus being the preacher . . . even when we preach: "When Christ is preached, Christ is preaching." That is to say, if this story is a model for our preaching, then a preacher would present Jesus (as the object of preaching) so that Jesus shows up as the preacher. Definitely, something new happens for preaching when Jesus enters the scene.

Beyond searching for examples in Scripture of the practice of preaching, we can consider a biblical response to the question, "On what basis do you preach?" by exploring actual words that are variously translated as "preaching."

Words Translated as "Preaching"

A common way to find out what the Bible has to say about topic X is to go to what is called a concordance. Searching for the word *preaching* is not necessarily as straightforward as one might think. Working with a concordance is helpful, but it can also be limiting, since multiple words in the original language have been translated as "preaching" and its various forms. We might miss some instances of preaching if we limit our search to that particular word. For example, each of the following actions could signify preaching: to tell the good news,[2] to cry or proclaim as a herald,[3] to bear witness,[4] to testify, to announce, to report.

First John 1:2 is an interesting example because it uses two different words for preaching: *martyroumen* and *apangellomen*. (Note the resonance of the second word with one who announces good news, an angel.)

> We declare to you what was from the beginning, what we have heard, what we have seen with our eyes, what we have looked at and touched with our hands, concerning the word of life—this life was revealed, and we have seen it and **testify to it** [*martyroumen*], and **declare** [*apangellomen*] to you the eternal life that was with the Father and was revealed to us—we **declare** [*apangellomen*] to you what we have seen and heard so that you also may have fellowship with us; and truly our fellowship is with the Father and with his Son Jesus Christ. (1 John 1:1–3)

You'll find forms of *apangellomen* in Matthew 28 ("So they left the tomb quickly with fear and great joy, and ran to tell [*apangeilei*] his disciples" [v. 8]) and John 20 ("Mary Magdalene went and announced to the disciples, 'I have seen the Lord'; and she told them [*angellousa*] that he had said these things to her" [v. 18]). Interestingly, only moments before that, Mary was conversing with two angels (*dyo angeles*) who appeared to her while she was weeping. And now she is "*angelous*-ing" to others. Consider the possibility of our proclamation as "angeling" (being angels for?) others.

Romans 10:15 employs two different words for "to proclaim." "And how are they to proclaim him unless they are sent? As it is written, 'How beautiful are the feet of those who bring good news!'" The first "proclaim" is from *kerrusso* and the second from *euaggelion*, the Greek word for "gospel." While the New Revised Standard Version wording is typical—"How beautiful are the feet of those who bring good news!"—this and other English translations miss the double use of *euangelizomenōn*: "How beautiful the feet of those proclaiming [*euangelizomenōn*] peace; of those proclaiming [*euangelizomenōn*] good news of good things." The double dose signifies its emphasis. The impact of preaching is not to be missed.

Clearly preaching is not simply speaking; something is happening. Also, that something is not just one thing; many things could happen.

Which word would you use to describe the preaching that happens in your communities? And why? Might a combination of what these words represent be a possibility for your preaching practices?

Having identified places in Scripture where people (including Peter, Paul, and Jesus himself) proclaim in ways that are similar to what we might describe as preaching, and by searching for words in the biblical language (Greek) that have been variously translated as "preaching" or "proclaiming," we discover that preaching is demonstrably an important ecclesial practice. But we also find possible models for preaching in Scripture where no one is actually preaching, and no word for "preaching" is used.

Regarding the latter, suppose one wants to find what Scripture might say about "workplace harassment." This phrase, as such, will not be found in a biblical concordance, but that doesn't mean the Bible has nothing to say about workplace harassment. To be sure, the Bible has much to say about how we treat one another in every environment. Similarly, we could and should broaden our search when it comes to preaching. Therefore, the next section includes instances that reflect the experience of a preaching event even apart from any activity we would recognize specifically as a preaching event.

Encounters with Jesus

In addition to places in Scripture where some form of preaching takes place or where preaching is specifically mentioned, we find biblical stories that feature an experience that is similar to a hoped-for experience of preaching, an encounter with Jesus.

I offer two examples, the woman at the well in John 4 and the disciples on the road to Emmaus in Luke 24. I encourage you to stop here and read the stories before proceeding. Then, in your own words, describe the characteristics of the encounter. The question before us is this: Might any of these characteristics guide our preaching practices so that they yield an encounter with Jesus?

I note the following characteristics in John 4 that might help us identify a biblical basis for why we preach as we do.

* Jesus, a Jew, dared to associate with a Samaritan.
* A very honest dialogue ensues between the woman and Jesus.
* Jesus offers something greater than the woman can imagine, and the woman questions it.

* Jesus reveals that he knows the woman's situation (regarding her previous husbands).
* The dialogue turns theological.
* Jesus reveals his true identity to the woman.
* Upon their return, the disciples question Jesus's choice to speak with a woman.
* After the encounter, the woman proclaims to her community that this one could be the Messiah.
* The woman invites others to "come and see" for themselves.
* People believe in Jesus because of the woman's testimony, and their hearing inspires them to see for themselves.

What do we learn about preaching from this encounter? Preaching, as an opportunity to facilitate an encounter with Jesus, might include dialogue, both among us and between us and God. Preaching might even provoke honest dialogue, with some people questioning what God is doing (a "living water" moment, of sorts). Preaching is certainly theological, as it facilitates a revealing of Jesus's true identity. Preaching might allow room for those who encounter Jesus to respond. Preaching could be about an encounter with the Messiah that compels us to invite others to "come and see" this one who truly knows us, thereby compelling others to have a similar experience.

If this story were to be our model for preaching, our preaching practices would be interactional and experiential. Our practices would move beyond where we typically consider preaching takes place and who we typically consider to be the preachers. We are not in the sanctuary; we are "at the well." We are not being led the witness of an upstanding citizen who has been given the right to speak by a community; we are being led by a woman who, despite having been marginalized because of her past, encounters Jesus and is compelled to invite others to "come and see." First, she witnesses. Then she bears witness. This story of one woman's encounter with Jesus seems to be an effective homiletical model: witnessing, bearing witness, hearing, and seeing for oneself.

Another story about an encounter with Jesus that might serve as a model for our preaching practice is recorded in Luke 24. Following the account of the men and women encountering the empty tomb, two of Jesus's disciples are making their way to Emmaus.

* The two disciples are walking and talking about all that had taken place.
* While they are walking and talking, Jesus starts to walk with them.
* Jesus's question about what they are talking about stops them in their tracks.
* The disciples' response is both sadness and surprise (has this man not heard the news?).
* That brief exchange leads one of the disciples to narrate a testimony about Jesus's greatness but admit his own disappointment that perhaps Jesus was not the one they had hoped for, since he is now dead.
* Jesus calls them out on their disbelief and explains to them "the things about himself in all the scriptures" beginning with "Moses and all the prophets" (v. 27).
* While they still don't have a clue that this man is Jesus, they are eager to invite him to stay with him.
* Jesus agrees to the invitation.
* They finally recognize Jesus when he takes bread, blesses and breaks it, and gives it to them.

* When Jesus "vanishe[s] from their sight," they begin to wonder, "Were not our hearts burning within us while he was talking to us on the road, while he was opening the scriptures to us?" (Luke 24:31–32).

What do we learn about preaching from this encounter? For starters, note that in verses 14 and 15, the words in Greek that have been translated as "talking" are *homiloun* and *homilein*. Sounds like our English word *homily*, right? From this encounter, we come to understand that *homily* means talking to one another, conversing. What happens when these two disciples are *homileo*-ing? Jesus appears. Again, the disciples' encounter with Jesus involves dialogue, both with one another and with Jesus. How does our preaching do that? How is preaching dialogue between us and Jesus as well as with one another? How is preaching an attempt to reveal Jesus's identity? (Of course, this story suggests, if *homileo*-ing doesn't "work," there is always the Eucharist!) Sometimes it is only when we look back, when we remember an experience, that we realize what we had a sense of at the time; "were not our hearts burning?" Maybe preaching helps us recognize our past encounters with Jesus along the way.

These two stories have challenged me to reconsider the notion that preaching primarily involves one person, often the called and ordained pastor, who serves as the sole biblical interpreter and proclaimer. That's not what we find in these stories. If our working definitions of preaching suggest that preaching is an encounter with Jesus, we will want to heed the details in these stories. Of course, these are not the only two stories in Scripture that might guide us, nor are they necessarily the most important. I encourage you to explore other biblical stories that narrate people's encounters with Jesus as we have done here. After considering the stories of, for example, the Syrophoenician woman, Nicodemus, and Mary in the garden, you might have an even sturdier biblical foundation upon which to build your community's preaching ministry.

Of course, other sections in Scripture offer a basis for our preaching as well. For example, the Bible exhorts disciples (and, by, extension, its readers and hearers) to "go therefore and make disciples of all nations" (Matt 28:19), essentially to share in the ministry of proclamation. Other verses further help us justify why we engage in this oral/aural practice of proclamation. For example, "So faith comes from what is heard, and what is heard comes through the word of Christ" (Rom 10:17). (This verse highlights why we don't simply send talking points to parishioners and call them a sermon.) But the biblical basis for our preaching doesn't start with Paul's letter to the Romans or even with the New Testament. It starts, "In the beginning. . . ."

The Theological Basis for Preaching

As this chapter has focused on a biblical basis for why we preach from the New Testament, you may have noticed the theological claims in that line of inquiry.

Before we move on to explicitly identifying a theological basis, take a moment to identify the things you know about God (or Jesus or the Holy Spirit) and how God acts in the world that have something to do with your community's preaching ministry.

1. _____

2. _____

3. _____

4. _____

Beyond the scope of events in the New Testament where preaching takes place and specific words that are translated as "preaching," and even beyond encounters with Jesus, we discover a theological basis for preaching. Notice what is happening in the following pericopes: "In the beginning when God created the heavens and the earth, the earth was a formless void and darkness covered the face of the deep, while a wind from God swept over the face of the waters. Then God said, 'Let there be light'; and there was light" (Gen 1:1–3). When God says, "Let there be light," there is light. Then again in verse 9, for example, when God says, "Let the waters," it is so. And so forth in Genesis. Indeed, when God speaks, something happens. God speaks creation into being.

The Psalms, too, tell of this creative speaking:

By the word of the Lord the heavens were made,
    and all their host by the breath of his mouth
He gathered the waters of the sea as in a bottle;
    he put the deeps in storehouses.
Let all the earth fear the Lord;
    let all the inhabitants of the world stand in awe of him.
For he spoke, and it came to be;
    he commanded, and it stood firm. (Ps 33:6–9)

"By the word of the Lord the heavens were made, and all their host by the breath of his mouth." When God speaks, something happens. "For he spoke, and it came to be; he commanded, and it stood firm." When God speaks, something happens. And then from Psalm 148, "Let them praise the name of the Lord, for he commanded and they were created" (v. 5).

We have a loquacious God (*Deus Loquens* was the phrase Martin Luther used for this notion) who creates through speaking. This loquaciously creative God invites creation (humans and "the heavens telling the Glory of God") to cocreate through speaking *viva vox evangelii*, the living voice of the gospel. "There was nothing until God spoke the Word," Elizabeth Achtemeier reminds. "And for us, too, there is the void, the chaos—the primevil *tohu wabbohu*, devoid of reality—until we speak the words. Human words, like God's Word, bring our universe into being and order, and perhaps the fact that we can speak and so create a world is the residual evidence that we were made in the image of God."[5]

Preaching, Achtemeier notes, is all about "the [immediate] action of God through the medium of human words."[6] God has chosen the medium of human words to impact God's beloved world. If you are inclined to question this choice, you would not be the first. Recall this dialogue:

> Moses said to the Lord, "Pardon your servant, Lord. I have never been eloquent, neither in the past nor since you have spoken to your servant. I am slow of speech and tongue."
>
> The Lord said to him, "Who gave human beings their mouths? Who makes them deaf or mute? Who gives them sight or makes them blind? Is it not I, the Lord? Now go; I will help you speak and will teach you what to say."
>
> But Moses said, "Pardon your servant, Lord. Please send someone else" (Exod 4:10–13 NIV).

Just as God is a speaking God, so too the church is a speaking church. Martin Luther insisted that the church is a mouth

41

house and not a pen house:[7] "And the Gospel should really not be something written, but a spoken word which brought forth the Scriptures, as Christ and the apostles have done. This is why Christ himself did not write anything but only spoke. He called his teaching not Scripture but Gospel, meaning good news or a proclamation that is spread not by pen but by word of mouth."[8]

Which is a more eventful experience for you: reading the score of a great symphony or hearing the symphony perform the score? While reading Scripture, even doing so silently, can affect us, hearing it is experiencing, as Charles Bartow calls it "*actio divina*"—that is, God's self-performance.[9] Unlike the role of literature, which according to T. S. Eliot is "to turn blood into ink," Bartow says the role of preaching is to turn ink (that is, the written word in the Bible) into blood (the oral proclamation of the word). This transformation, through human words in preaching, is *actio divina*, God's self-performance.

Preaching's emphasis on orality/aurality requires present-tense proclamation. God, Emmanuel, is with us . . . here, now, through *this* word: "We cannot present the biblical story as something that has happened only in the past, recounting the event, and admiring God's marvelous deeds long ago, or even tacking on a few deduced applications to the present. If God's actions are not done now also for us through the sermon, they are of antiquarian interest only and are even goads to our hopelessness. God may have loved us once; the question is, Does he love us now?"[10]

We maintain this oral/aural event because of who God is and what God does. This same chatty, creative God is the incarnate word with us, Emmanuel (God-with-us). In John 1, we hear (!) that the word, the *logos*, is still an active agent in creation.

But now the word is not just something spoken by the divine; the divine *is* the word. What does it mean now that a word has turned into a person, Jesus? There is something about the spoken word that defines Christianity and shapes its practices; this is a foundational theological commitment that shapes our preaching practices too.

> *In what way(s) are theological themes such as* logos, *incarnation,* Emmanuel, deus loquens, *and* viva vox evangelii *at work for you as you substantiate your preaching practices?*
>
> *What additional theological themes are at work?*

A good resource to assist in responding to these questions is one's denominational library of resources. Here one should be able to find an ecclesiological basis for preaching.

The Ecclesiological Basis for Preaching

If you are unsure what your denomination says about preaching in your church, you are not alone. A good place to start your search is with your church's defining documents. As you do, try not to get frustrated when you go searching and cannot find clear statements on why we preach the way we do. It is not uncommon to discover that as much emphasis as numerous Christian denominations place on preaching, they are less clear about identifying the basis for its practice. Perhaps the benefit of this lack of information is that we may now have the freedom to make our practice align with what we claim, and vice versa. It also means that perhaps we are in the serendipitous position to make our denominational claims about preaching clearer (which is, I hope, a valuable by-product of this book).

I'll offer here an example to get you started by focusing on the tradition with which I'm most familiar—Lutheranism. If someone were to ask me what "my church" says about preaching, I would begin by identifying denominational resources. My brainstormed list of conversation partners would include the following:

* the Bible
* the Creeds
* *Luther's Works*
* *The Book of Concord* (including the Augsburg Confession)
* the constitution and bylaws of the Evangelical Lutheran Church in America (ELCA)
* *The Use of the Means of Grace: A Statement on the Practice of Word and Sacrament* (adopted "for guidance and practice" at the ELCA Churchwide Assembly in 1997)
* *Principles for Worship* (a complementary resource to *The Use of the Means of Grace* emerging from a series of "Renewing Worship" consultations in 2001 that develops principles and supporting materials to address four particular dimensions of the church's worship: language, music, preaching, and worship space)
* ordination vows

The list is not meant to be exhaustive, but it's a good start. The next step is to determine (1) if the item is authoritative or guiding and (2) what in the document validates (and perhaps even critiques) "the way we've always done it." I'll begin with the last bullet point because, while a liturgical rite is not necessarily an authoritative "document," it does point to what might be authoritative. Here is an excerpt from the ELCA's ordination rite: "The church in which you are to be ordained confesses that the *holy scriptures* are the word of God and are the norm of its faith and life. We accept, teach, and confess the Apostles', the Nicene, and the Athanasian *Creeds*. We also acknowledge the *Lutheran confessions* as true witnesses and faithful expositions of the holy scriptures. Will you therefore preach and teach in accordance with the holy scriptures and these creeds and confessions? . . . Will you be diligent in your study of the holy scriptures and faithful in your *use of the means of grace*?" (italics added). Candidates for ordination for both Word and Sacrament and Word and Service ministries in the ELCA are to respond to these questions, "I will, and I ask God to help me." For me, the vow I made on July 19, 1998, makes it authoritative.

Note the correspondence between my brainstormed list and the authorities mentioned in the vows. An item that is not named in the vows but is on my list is *Luther's Works*, a compendium of extant lectures, writings, sermons, and the like of Martin Luther, the namesake of the tradition. There is a wide range of viewpoints on the authoritative nature of Luther's works for the various Lutheran denominations. Just because an author identifies with a denomination does not mean that person's article or book is a "denominational document." (For example, this book is not an authoritative Lutheran document even though I, a Lutheran, am the author.) The same can be said about Luther for the contemporary Lutheran church. Luther, of course, was not a Lutheran. He was a Roman Catholic monk, priest, and professor whose challenges to his denomination sparked a reformation in the sixteenth century. While the ELCA ordination vows do not ask the ordinand to subscribe to Luther as authoritative, it is worth asking to what extent one's Lutheran denomination (there is much variety, since the global communion called the Lutheran World Federation includes 148 Lutheran churches) subscribes to Luther's writings as authoritative.[11]

So while Luther is not irrefutably authoritative, some Lutherans heed his writings on preaching as a guide, especially when they are claiming that God is the agent of efficacious preaching and preaching "is the medium through which salvation is bestowed."[12] Through the work of the Holy Spirit, Christ himself shows up to declare forgiveness of sins and salvation: "It is easy enough for someone to preach the word to me, but only God can put it into my heart. He must speak it in my heart, or nothing at all will come of it. If God remains silent, the final effect is as though nothing had been said."[13] In other words, preachers "must assume the 'right to speak,' though not the 'power to accomplish.'"[14] Luther recognized God's decision to invite humans to participate in this event: "It is God's good pleasure to shine his Word in the heart with law and gospel, but not without the external, spoken Word. What an office, a name and an honor of preaching to be 'God's co-workers' to achieve his purpose!"[15]

My list (and the ordination vows) include the Bible, the three creeds, and the Lutheran Confessions (found in *The Book of Concord*). The Bible—in my opinion, the most authoritative item on the list—was already addressed above. And while the three creeds do not necessarily offer guidance on why or how we preach, they do offer the central content of our preaching. The Lutheran confessions found in *The Book of Concord*, however, have much to say about why we preach. The Augsburg Confession, in particular, is key: "To obtain such faith God instituted the office of preaching, giving the gospel and the sacraments. Through these, as through means, he gives the Holy Spirit, who produces faith, where and when he wills, in those who hear the Gospel. It teaches that we have a gracious God, not through our merit but through Christ's merit, when we so believe."[16] The

Scriptures and our Confessions establish this purpose of preaching. We believe that "through the Word and the sacraments, as through means, the Holy Spirit is given, and the Holy Spirit produces faith, where and when it pleases God, in those who hear the Gospel."[17] Preaching, as it turns out, affects the whole church because, indeed, it creates the church. When God speaks, something happens.

The ELCA's statement of purpose says it is committed to "worship God in proclamation of the Word and administration of the sacraments and through lives of prayer, praise, thanksgiving, witness, and service."[18] It is significant that the first item listed in the section outlining how the church "participate[s] in God's mission" is to note that the church shall "proclaim God's saving Gospel of justification by grace for Christ's sake through faith alone, according to the apostolic witness in the Holy Scripture, preserving and transmitting the Gospel faithfully to future generations."[19] Preaching is a priority.

Regarding the role of the rostered leaders and their relationship to preaching, the constitution is clear: "Consistent with the faith and practice of the Evangelical Lutheran Church in America, every minister of Word and Sacrament shall preach the Word."[20] And again, every minister of Word and Service is to "be rooted in the Word of God, for proclamation and service."[21] For both leadership rosters, preaching or proclamation is prioritized.

Every generation has had to interpret Scripture and the confessions in its own context. "The Formula of Concord" in *The Book of Concord* is such an attempt by the generation immediately after Luther's death. In the late twentieth century, one of those interpretive documents, *The Use of the Means of Grace*, was drafted in the ELCA.[22] The priority on and the sacramental nature of preaching are unmistakable in this document: "By the power of the Spirit, this very Word of God, which is Jesus Christ, is read in the Scriptures, proclaimed in preaching, announced in the forgiveness of sins, eaten and drunk in the Holy Communion, and encountered in the bodily presence of the Christian community. By the power of the Spirit active in Holy Baptism, this Word washes a people to be Christ's own Body in the world. We have called this gift of Word and Sacrament by the name 'the means of grace.'"[23]

The Use of the Means of Grace served as the guiding document for Renewing Worship, a denomination-wide effort to "invite study and response, encourage unity, and foster common understanding and practice."[24] Neither the Renewing Worship consultations nor the *Principles for Worship* were meant to "impose uniformity."[25] This document is especially helpful as it outlines a variety of principles, applications of those principles, and their background.

Principles for Worship contains an entire section on preaching: "In a time when new forms of communication continue to emerge, preaching still holds a prominent place in the church's worship as a means of conveying the word of God. Preaching is a matter of great interest not only to those who prepare and deliver sermons week by week, but also to those who participate in preaching by listening and receiving the word, week in and week out."[26] A few principles are worth highlighting for our purposes here.

> Principle P-2: "God calls the whole people of God to proclaim the living word in worship, in witness, and in lives shaped by freedom in Christ."[27]
> Principle P-5: "The word of God is first of all a spoken word [Gen 1; John 1:11], an event that

bears the power to create and to transform. Preaching participates in the creating and transforming power of God's word."[28]

Principle P-10: "The authority of preaching is, in part, an extension of Jesus' own mission of preaching the reign of God. The authority of preaching is a servant authority, rooted in the mercy of God and is bestowed by the one who 'humbled himself, taking the form of a servant.'"[29]

Additionally, Principle P-17 emphasizes that "preaching uses the tools of human communication to convey the message of divine grace."[30]

Before moving on, take some time to explore your congregation's guiding documents to understand what definition(s) of preaching are operational. Does your congregational constitution or bylaws say anything about preaching? What does your pastor's "letter of call" say about preaching? And then broaden the scope of your research by asking these questions about your denomination.[31]

Our reasons for preaching (and for preaching as we do) are biblical, theological, and ecclesiological. (Feel free to add other reasons in your exploration.) Why do we preach? We preach because we vow to do so. Why do we vow to do so? Because our church asks us to do so. Why does the church ask us to do so? God asks the church to do so in order that the church might continue God's mission in the world God so loves. God still speaks through our proclamation. And when God speaks, something happens.

For Reflection and Discussion

1. What biblical stories serve as a basis for the way your community practices preaching?
2. Describe God's (Jesus's, the Holy Spirit's) involvement in your community's preaching practices.
3. How does preaching in your community align (or not) with your denomination's commitments to and recommendations for preaching?
4. What would you say if someone were to ask you today, "Why preach?"
5. In light of your answer to question 4, will you want to amend your working definition of preaching or your community's preaching practice so that they are more aligned with your biblical, theological, and denominational basis for preaching?

3

The Case for Collaboration

The women in Zimbabwe shared the load as they came back from the well. Their morning ritual of getting water was graced with full-voiced singing as they walked side by side down the red soil road. No woman carried her own bucket. Instead, each woman assisted another woman by holding a side of her bucket as she was helped by yet another woman holding one side of her bucket. With this colaboring plan, each woman carried half the load of two buckets instead of the full load of one bucket. "Let's try it," I nudged my companions as we walked along another road later that day with bags of groceries. Regrettably, it had not occurred to us to share the load of the grocery bags. But when we did, it felt like we were bearing less than half the weight. How could that be? Our collaboration gave us a spring in our step.

If you want to go fast, go alone.
If you want to go far, go together.

—African proverb

In what arenas of your life do you colabor with others? in your family unit? In school? At work? In music rehearsal? On sports teams? We collaborate as communities in preparation for floods and after tornados and wildfires. Government entities collaborate during state and national crises. Think of a time when you were in the midst of a collaborative project and the experience felt just right. What was it like? Describe the project and your feelings.

In the eighteenth and nineteenth centuries, communities came together for "barn raising," during which community members would help build a barn for a particular homestead. They would do so without pay, knowing that the effort might someday be reciprocated. This similar collaborative attitude is called the "raising bee" in England and *talkoot* in Finland. In East Africa, the Swahili word for this concept and practice, *harambee*, literally means "all pull together." ("Harambee" is Kenya's motto and appears on its coat of arms.) In France, the *charrette* emerged in the nineteenth century at Paris's École des Beaux-Arts (School of Fine Arts). A team of urban planners would engage in an intense period of designing with all stakeholders (not just paid professionals but those who would be affected by the design) to solve a planning problem by developing a new design. They would work feverishly right up until the deadline, at which point the *charrette* (cart or chariot) would collect their models for review. *Charrettes* are still common in urban planning, where stakeholders (developers and residents) come together for full-day or multiday events.

I am recommending that we consider preaching more in terms of these cooperative efforts where all stakeholders colabor with one another. This commitment to a more collaborative preaching ministry has been recommended by others for many decades but still has not found its way to regular practice. I am surprised by this, since in a number of ways, Christians have adopted collaboration in many of their theories and practices. For example, the Christian church's understanding of mission has for the most part shifted to a model that is more about accompaniment than an effort to yield "converts."[1] Shared power and mutuality are key in mission work. The field of biblical studies, too, values and promotes communal interpretation as guided by the story in Acts in which "the Ethiopian eunuch realizes, interpretation happens best through conversation with others."[2] Given Tom Long's claim that preaching preparation *is* ministry (as opposed to simply preparation *for* ministry), we will want to articulate what we mean by ministry. What ecclesiology (from the Greek word *ekklesia* meaning church) undergirds our practices?

An article in a recent Episcopal seminary magazine features interviews with a number of bishops. They responded to the question, "How has your thinking about leadership formation changed?"[3] Note the collaborative ecclesiology at work.

* Rev. Isaiah "Shaneequa" Brokenleg, Episcopal Staff Officer for Racial Reconciliation: "I think we're seeing leadership as more facilitation and organizing. I liken it to being a midwife. You're there to help give birth to whatever's happening, and you're not there to control it because that's not your role."

* Rt. Rev. Carlye Hughes, Bishop of Newark: "What is most helpful is when people enter with a posture of

being willing to learn and willing to try things, and what is not helpful is when people enter into ordained ministry thinking they have to know all of the answers."

* Rev. Deon Johnson, Bishop of Missouri: "When we look at our spiritual ancestors, when we look at Jesus, he sent disciples out in twos. One of the things that we're beginning to experiment with in the diocese of Missouri is a regional model. The deacon, the priest, and the lay folks work in conjunction, looking at the area rather than just this specific congregation."

* Rt. Rev. Gretchen Rehberg, Bishop of Spokane: "We've inherited a model where the priest is viewed as the one who does everything, and that model can't survive. We need to see it as a partnership, and we're not providing equivalent lay leadership formation."

* Rt. Rev. Susan Brown Snook, Bishop of San Diego: "Ordained leadership is not anymore about waiting in your study and crafting a lovely sermon. . . . People need to understand what that good news is for them and for their neighborhoods. They need to learn how to proclaim it. Not all of us are gifted one-on-one evangelists but all of us should be able to lead a community that proclaims the good news, that gets out into the neighborhoods, and respond to the needs that we see there."

Leadership in a collaborative ecclesiology reflects the commitments of community organizers more than those of a hierarchical organization.[4] Community organizing, according to former US president Barack Obama, is "grassroots work that [brings] ordinary people together around issues of local concern."[5] Obama marshaled the principles of organizing both to run his campaign and to govern as president. One of the primary principles of community organizing Obama names is "to encourage participation and active citizenship among those who'd been left out, and to teach them not just to trust their elected leaders, but to trust one another, and themselves."[6] We're back to barn raising. "Harambee." Community organizers often quote Brazilian Catholic archbishop Dom Hélder Pessoa Câmara: "If I dream alone, it is only a dream. If we dream together, it is the beginning of reality."[7]

The phrase "collaborative ecclesiology" actually seems redundant, since *ekklesia* inherently suggests a community, the church, a group of "co-laborers" (*synergoi*): "We are coworkers [*synergoi*] with God; you are God's farm, God's building" (1 Cor 3:9 IB). Some churches know this concept in their bones and live it. "Teología en conjunto" is the way Hispanic protestant churches engage in theology together, paralleling the biblical concept of *mishpahah* ("the clan, tribe or extended family").[8]

In so many ways, the church embraces collaboration, but unfortunately, not in our preaching practices, even though (1) it is where we are and (2) it is who we are.

It's Where We Are

Nature's collaborative ecosystem was hard at work well before we came along. Ecology writer Michael Allaby notes, "If I were asked to identify a single principle that seems to guide the development of life on Earth, I would have to call it collaboration, the establishment of mutually supportive communities."[9] Forests, for example, are "vast, ancient and intricate societ[ies]" in which there is "negotiation, reciprocity and perhaps even selflessness." University of British Columbia forest ecology professor

Suzanne Simard speaks of forests as mycorrhizal networks in which everything is "so thoroughly connected, communicative and codependent that some scientists have described [forests] as superorganisms."[10] A grove of aspen trees is particularly illustrative. What appears to be numerous individual trees is actually one single organism that can stretch to one hundred acres. The extensive root system of this aspen clonal colony collaborates with other species as well. For example, just inside the aspen's thin outer layer of bark is a green photosynthetic layer that provides nutrients for other animals.

Geese know about colaboring too. You've seen it before—a wedge of geese flying in a *V* formation. While one might say the bird in the front of the *V* is the leader, that bird is there only temporarily, since leadership rotates. Each bird takes a turn occupying different roles, including the front of the *V*. Leadership gurus, even in the church, have noticed this kind of colaboring. Church leadership authors encourage ministry leaders to be more like those high-flying geese with regard to role-sharing.[11] I can't help but wonder what a kind of "front of the *V*" rotation might be like with regard to our preaching practices.

If the wisdom of geese doesn't convince us to consider new options, perhaps bees will, since bees, too, collaborate to fulfill multiple roles for the sake of the colony's well-being. In their brief lifetime (only one to seven months), bees "cycle through fifteen to twenty tasks, including cleaning, brood tending, Queen tending, comb building, food handling, ventilation, guard duty, orientation flights and foraging."[12] Bees live in colonies and work in a highly collaborative manner. They need one another to stay alive.

Business consultant David Zinger collaborated with a beekeeping professor of philosophy and an artist who creates art with honeybees to "look at what could be learned about human collaboration from studying bees." They've discovered that bees "ensur[e] there is someone ready or being trained for every role and function in [an] organization to make transitions seamless." In the same way that honeybees pollinate profusely while gathering nectar from outside the hive, he advises, "reach out beyond your hive, collaborating with others as you share and gather new ideas from everywhere."[13] Thomas Seeley, author of *Honeybee Democracy*, comments on the move from "me to we" in the work world: "By operating without a leader the scout bees of a swarm neatly avoid one of the greatest threats to good decision making by groups: a domineering leader. Such an individual reduces a group's collective power to uncover a diverse set of possible solutions to a problem, to critically appraise these possibilities, and to winnow out all but the best one."[14]

Not only might humans consider collaborating *like* bees, but we would do well to collaborate *with* bees, since the survival of bees is linked to the survival of humans. Melittologist (one who studies wild bees) Laurence Packer says, "If all bees died out, there would be worldwide food shortages and perhaps one-quarter of the human population would starve."[15]

Perhaps what I am suggesting here in relation to preaching is a form of biomimicry, which, in biologist Janine M. Benyus's terms, is "conscious emulation of life's genius." It is the "practice of applying lessons from nature to the invention of healthier, more sustainable technologies for people." Biomimetic designers (called "biomimics") "focus on understanding, learning from, and emulating the strategies used by living things, with the intention of creating designs and technologies that are sustainable."[16] Benyus's book *Biomimicry: Innovation Inspired by Nature* "documents many teams of scientists seeking to understand and emulate nature's building secrets."[17] I wonder if a kind of biomimetic homiletic is in our future.

It's Who We Are

It turns out that humans, too, are "hardwired for connection." But what does that really mean? Amy Banks, MD, instructor of psychiatry at Harvard Medical School, responds to this exact question: "Neuroscience is confirming that our nervous systems want us to connect with other human beings. . . . There have been studies that look at emotions in human beings such as disgust, shame, happiness, where the exact same areas of the brain light up in the listener who is reading the feelings of the person talking. We are, literally, hardwired to connect."[18]

Our brains have a built-in "collaborative awareness," which is defined as "two or more entities working in concert to create a continuous and nearly instant feedback loop of group knowledge, adaptability and growth" and is a function of what some call our "connected brain."[19] When our connected brains are prioritized in life, our creativity, productivity, and resilience increase. Some neuroscientists have proposed that the foundational human need is not physiological, as Abraham Maslow (of Maslow's hierarchy of human needs fame) claimed. It's "being socially connected and cared for."[20] Matthew D. Lieberman—social neuroscientist at the University of California, Los Angeles, and author of the book *Social: Why Our Brains Are Wired to Connect*—is one who has challenged Maslow's claim, since Lieberman's studies show that the brain's "free time is devoted to thinking socially."[21]

What all mammalian infants, from tree shrews to human babies, really need from the moment of birth is a caregiver who is committed to making sure that the infant's biological needs are met. . . . Without social support, infants will never survive to become adults who can provide for themselves . . . this restructuring of Maslow's pyramid tells us something critical about "who we are." Love and belonging might seem like a convenience we can live without, but our biology is built to thirst for connection because it is linked to our most basic survival needs. . . . Our need for connection is the bedrock upon which the others are built.[22]

When we are connecting to others and doing things we enjoy, our brains actually release what some call "happy hormones," such as dopamine, oxytocin (sometimes referred to as the "cuddle hormone"), and serotonin. These chemicals cause us to feel a surge of positive emotion. Neurotransmitters such as endorphins make us feel euphoric, much like the "runner's high," and inhibit pain. When we are disconnected, on the other hand, "when we experience social pains or feel the distress of withheld social connection," we can hardly "focus on much else until this need is met."[23] Banks explains this "relational neurobiology" with the social pain overlap theory (SPOT), which identifies an overlap between social and physical pain: "The distress of social pain is biologically identical to the distress of physical pain. Most people in our culture understand that physical pain is a major stressor, but we often reject the idea of social pain. This impacts our society on a grand scale; for example look at instances of racism or homophobia—any of the ways that we stratify and divide our social structures can literally cause pain."[24] Lieberman's research on the human brain shows that social pain is experienced through the same neural pathways used to process physical pain. It is no wonder that when we experience loss, social rejection, or disconnection, we use physiological explanations such as "She broke my heart," "He hurt my feelings," or "That felt like being punched in the gut."

Adopting Collaboration

Suffice it to say, connection and collaboration are beneficial for our wholeness and well-being and among the reasons I want to imagine the possibility of shaping our ecclesiastical practices, in particular our preaching practices, so that they encourage the collaboration for which we are hardwired. Do I think collaborative preaching processes will "cure" the social ills of our time? Hardly. But do I think facilitating more opportunities for collaboration where and when possible will benefit us all? Yes. There is nothing inherent in Christian proclamation that keeps us from collaborating more in our preaching practices.

Other industries, disciplines, and arenas have embraced the collaborative nature of where we are and who we are. What can we learn from them? I take my cue for this interdisciplinary foray into cultural arenas that have embraced collaboration as a key framework from a trusted authority. Jesus looks to *the everyday* to assist him in his mission. Jesus asks us to pay attention to the mustard seeds, fig trees, and varieties of soil for life lessons. He invites us to consider birds, lilies, and stray sheep. He leads us to various work sites such as seashores, vineyards, pastures, and marketplaces to learn about discipleship, vocation, and the kingdom of God. He gathers with people for conversation by sycamore trees at night, by wells in broad daylight, and in gardens near empty tombs, so that we might come to know Jesus's true identity and develop a relationship with him. For Jesus, it seems, all of life holds potential for theological exploration and discovery.

I am also reminded of the bishop of Hippo, Augustine (354–430 CE), who, in what is considered the first handbook of Christian rhetoric, *On Christian Doctrine*, endorsed the use of whatever is available for the sake of the gospel.[25] Conversation with, borrowing from, and getting curious about various disciplines and arenas are "fair game."[26] It is this kind of interdisciplinary work that can lead to innovation, creativity, productivity, problem-solving, and even our well-being.

Lieberman's work noted above outlines the fascinating neurological evidence for the primacy of social connections in our lives and encourages us to use this information in our workplaces and schools and for our personal and social well-being.[27] I see evidence of this in education, technology, and the arts, three arenas that can activate our imaginations for more collaborative preaching practices.

Education

You've heard it said, and maybe you've said it yourself, "It's never too late to learn." Indeed, the "neuronal makeup of our brains is far more flexible than previously believed." Thanks to neuroscientists like Liz Gould, we now know that "new neurons can be born in adulthood."[28] Even more, this process can be stimulated with exercise (i.e., learning by doing). The authors of *Make It Stick: The Science of Successful Learning* agree that learning is deeper and more durable when it is effortful: "Learning that's easy is like writing in the sand, here today and gone tomorrow."[29] They argue that trying to solve a problem *before being taught the solution* leads to better learning, even when errors are made in the attempt.

As it turns out, psychological research has shown that focused work, not the absence of work, creates optimal experiences. While one might assume "we will be happiest when we have nothing to do—lying in a backyard hammock, sunning ourselves at the beach, or just vegging out on the couch," psychologist Mihaly Csikszentmihalyi found that "optimal experiences" for humans "usually occur when a person's body or mind is stretched to its limits in a voluntary effort to accomplish something difficult and worthwhile."[30]

Effortful, focused, hands-on work leads to fruitful and memorable learning. I've got this kind of learning in mind as I think about leading Bible study and preaching. Does the way we currently go about our preaching practices reflect effortful, focused, hands-on work? For the pastor, yes. But what about for others? When we wonder why some in our congregation aren't as biblically literate as we would hope, we might want to reconsider our dependence on a fifteen-minute sermon with one person speaking to a crowd of people as a primary occasion for people to learn *about* the Bible.

We've also come to know that learning occurs when we collaborate, teach, and learn from peers: "We ought to be doing much more peer learning, particularly age-staggered learning. . . . The teacher then becomes a coach helping to teach the 12-year-old, and the 14-year-old will reap the benefits of prosocial learning."[31] I think here of the proposal for preachers to equip others to preach, at least to teach others the practices they've learned to interpret the Bible. One person telling another person what the Bible means (that action alone is worth questioning) without teaching the skills of biblical interpretation will not lead to learning.

The social aspect of learning is not extraneous. As a preacher, I've wanted to implement the "active exchange of ideas" in "collaborative learning small groups" in order to both increase participant interest and promote critical thinking. I've wanted to incorporate the evidence that "cooperative teams achieve at higher levels of thought and retain information longer than students who work quietly as individuals."[32] I am also moved by the way schools have appropriated the evidence that an increased sense of belonging is linked to a higher grade point average (GPA); they are beginning to "encourage better social climates where students feel like they belong."[33] I wonder if our congregations might do the same (that is, "encourage better social climates," not the GPA part) even, and especially, with our quintessential practices, such as worship, Bible study, and preaching.

Technology

Every day most of us hold in our hands evidence that the concept of collaboration has changed the "tech world," which has changed how we live in the world. We are no longer passive receivers of information; we are active participants: "The smartphone also enhances the participatory culture by increased levels of interactivity. Instead of merely watching, users are actively involved in making decisions, navigating pages, contributing their own content and choosing what links to follow."[34] Even our roles as consumers have shifted from being passive receivers to active contributors.

People in the technology industry work toward "enabling participation," because they recognize we are fully immersed in "participatory culture." In a participatory culture, people have "strong support for creating and sharing one's creations with others," "believe that their contributions matter," and "feel some degree of social connection with one another (at the very least, they care what other people think about what they have created)."[35] Participatory culture does not mean that every member has to contribute, "but all must believe they are free to contribute when ready and that what they contribute will be appropriately valued."[36]

Technology enables its users to be content producers. Younger people embrace this world; it's where they are. But it's not just young people. We are all fully immersed in the wiki era. Mass collaboration, or crowdsourcing, "relies on free individual agents to come together and cooperate to improve a given operation or solve a problem."[37]

Ask the "gamers" in your ministry setting how technology's "participatory culture" relies on collaboration. If we weren't wired for connection before (though we were), it is unavoidable now. In a whole new way, it's where we are and it's who we are. If this is our world, but then we are seemingly just passive recipients when we come to worship (and in particular, the time for the sermon), there is a disconnect between this experience and the rest of our lives, even our own physiological makeup. I think this disconnect is a surmountable missed opportunity.

The Arts

In the performing arts, there is a live interaction between "performer" and "audience," a form of participation. Some people even say that performers and audience members are collaborating to make meaning.[38] While the word *audience* itself assumes the primacy of hearing (think: audio, auditor), communication theorists have helped us understand that an audience member is not a passive listener.[39] Wilbur Schramm, the founder of the field of communication studies, admits, "The most dramatic change in general communication theory during the last forty years has been the gradual abandonment of the idea of a passive audience, and its replacement by the concept of a highly active, highly selective audience, manipulating rather than being manipulated by a message."[40]

Performance theorist Ronald Pelias's work on audiences is helpful. He claims that audience members' list of responsibilities includes understanding and performing their roles as sense makers and evaluators. As sense maker, the ideal audience member remains open, is ready to enter the communicative exchange, is receptive to the aesthetic communication the performer offers, and can adopt a stance. The audience's responsibility is to strive for understanding. As evaluator, the audience-as-performer provides description, judgment (i.e., critique), and justification for one's judgment. Regarding the latter, not just any judgment will be appropriate; audience members as evaluators must recognize their rationale for such evaluative remarks.[41]

As both sense makers and evaluators, audience-as-performers recognize cues from performers and events themselves in order to adopt an appropriate stance, have the ability to question their stance midperformance, maintain engagement with aesthetic events in order to gain competence, assume an ideal psychological stance by freeing oneself from preconceptions and personal biases, hold judgment in check, and acquire and utilize careful listening skills. Indeed, Pelias gives the audience leading roles; they are primary actors in aesthetic events.

Another performance theorist, Baz Kershaw, asserts that "the totally passive audience is a figment of the imagination; a practical impossibility," since "the reactions of audiences influence the nature of the performance." He observes, "It is not simply that the audience affects emotional tone or stylistic nuance: the spectator is engaged fundamentally in the active construction of meaning as a performance event proceeds. In this sense performance is 'about' the transaction of meaning, a continuous negotiation between stage and auditorium to establish the significance of the signs and conventions through which they interact."[42]

The work of Pelias and Kershaw is useful as we think about the collaborative roles of performer and audience. Some performance artists have gone a step further as they have expanded the role of audience to coperformer.

THEATRE IN THE ROUND

In the proscenium performance space, the stage is in front with nearly every member of the audience having a similar view. The "fourth wall" is an imaginary line that separates the stage and auditorium. The audience can see through this fourth wall, of course, and the actors are not to turn their back on the audience members who are on the other side of that fourth wall. However, with the advent of "theatre in the round," the configuration of "the furniture" changes.[43] The fourth wall is removed and the distance between performer and audience is reduced. An actor's back will inevitably be turned to some part of the audience. While the actor may not be able to see all members of the audience, the audience will always be able to see the actor, thus precipitating a shift in power. The "politics" of engagement changes. Just as there is no front or back seat when people are gathered at a round table, this kind of staging in a performance has an equalizing effect, which potentially gives people a greater sense that their contributions matter, noted above as one of the important elements of participatory culture.

Theatre of the Oppressed

Students of Brazilian theatre director Augusto Boal take the performer-audience dynamic to a whole new level. In the 1960s, Boal, highly influenced by Paulo Freire's *Pedagogy of the Oppressed*, developed a theatre experience where audience members would stop a performance in order to suggest a different action for "the character experiencing oppression." The actor would then do what the audience member suggested. At one such performance, a woman got so frustrated when the actor did not understand her suggestion that she went onto the stage herself to show them what she meant: "For Boal this was the birth of the spect-actor (not spectator) and his theatre was transformed. He began inviting audience members with suggestions for change onto the stage to demonstrate their ideas. In so doing, he discovered that through this participation the audience members became empowered not only to imagine change but to actually practice that change, reflect collectively on the suggestion, and thereby become empowered to generate social action."[44]

Now active in over seventy countries, Theatre of the Oppressed is "a format of theatre activities and performances that engages communities in social change." Communities are invited to be active participants in that change—first in a performance forum as a kind of rehearsal for the forum of life. Spectators have become "spect-actors" so they might rehearse being agents of change in the world.[45]

In the case noted above, not only is "audience" a "performer," but "performers" also recognize their role as "audience." So too in preaching. Preachers aid listeners' listening when they are aware of their own roles as both performer and audience. As author Robin Meyers asserts, "How better to regard the ears of others than to begin with a regard for one's own."[46] While I'm not quite ready to suggest that congregation members replace the preacher in the middle of the sermon, I am wondering how they can more actively participate in the cocreation of sermons, before and after the sermon certainly, but perhaps even during.[47]

FILM

Film is not a live performance, of course, but the industry has figured out that collaboration with the viewers has benefits. In 2018 the creators of the Netflix television series *Black Mirror* decided to crowdsource ideas for the trajectory of an episode. The episode ended up becoming a stand-alone film entitled *Bandersnatch*. In a kind of "choose-your-own-adventure," viewers make choices as they are viewing the film, and the film proceeds accordingly. (Apparently, there are over one trillion possible paths the viewer can take.) One film critic remarks, "In eliminating the passivity and creating an interactive experience in which viewers are involved and culpable, Netflix has created a multi-dimensional piece of art. On top of all the perceptions we bring to our viewing experiences (what we think of the leading actor, the mood we're in when we watch, what we think of *Black Mirror*), there are added layers of nuance to each session."[48]

Even for artists not willing to go that far, filmmakers, like live stage performers, are interested in the effect their creative work has on viewers: "The filmmaker organizes shots, camera movement, editing, and music to elicit certain reactions so that viewers will respond right on cue precisely as intended."[49] In the last decade, this desire for impact has been taken to a new level with the development of a new filmmaking role in a film's credits, the "impact producer," who is responsible "for maximizing a film's potential for social change."[50] With audience participation in mind, the company Imagine Impact (launched in 2018 by Brian Grazer, Ron Howard, and Tyler Mitchell) created an "open submission process," in order to "identify and develop feature film ideas in four specific genres over the next year that they will then bring to Netflix. . . . Imagine Impact was launched . . . as a means of accelerating and democratizing the script development process by attempting to remove bias from the submission process allowing the writer's voice to speak for itself and the most viable projects to move forward, regardless of the applicant's location, demographic or representation status."[51]

I wonder if our congregations would do well to create impact teams in order to maximize a sermon's potential for social change.[52]

Primed for Collaboration

My hope is that the church's practices—in particular, preaching—can take a cue from the ways people in these other disciplines and arenas have come to terms with and even embraced the fact that collaboration is where we are and who we are. We in the church are also hardwired for collaboration. We do not often adapt quickly, but as the African proverb asserts, together we go far. Preaching, one of the church's primary practices, is not exempt from colaboring efforts. Collaboration is what we do as humans—so too as God's beloved body of Christ, the church, *ekklesia*. Even in our preaching practices, we have an opportunity to embrace the collaborative nature of where we are and who we are.

For Reflection and Discussion

1. Do you have any other examples of the collaborative ecosystems of the natural world? In other words, where do you see creation's collaborative spirit at work?

2. Who in your communities might be your conversation partner(s) in order to understand how we humans are hardwired to connect?

3. Describe other arenas that you know of or that you participate in that have embraced collaboration.

4. In what ways does your congregation's ecclesiology embrace collaboration?

5. How might collaborative commitments explored in this chapter be fulfilled in your congregation's preaching ministry?

4

Feedforward

Collaborative Sermon Preparation

Now that you have established a working definition of preaching that takes into consideration the basis on which one preaches and to what end, and have explored the value of collaboration, we turn to the "how" of collaborative preaching. As you make your way through this section, be mindful of the way the *what* and *why* might shape the *how* of your preaching. For example, if one believes that preaching should create space for an encounter with the living Christ but preaches in a way that seeks to persuade people into religious assent, the disconnect will be evident. Or, if one says that preaching is how God imbues God's grace, then preaching probably should include present-tense, second-person speech and explicitly name God as a primary actor. If one's reason to preach reflects a sense that humans participate in God's creative activity through speaking, then preaching would do well to mirror such human/divine collaboration. Directly to the point of this book, if ministry is understood to be collaborative, and preaching is ministry, then sermon preparation should be the work of the community together rather than the work of one person.

Some people think a collaborative approach to preaching is a new thing. However, chapter 2 identified a number of homiletics professors who have proposed a collaborative approach to sermon preparation. Lucy Atkinson Rose identifies examples that go back to the mid-twentieth century: "To facilitate dialogue between the preacher and the congregation, [Clyde] Reid suggests pre-sermon Bible study groups and post-sermon discussion groups. Gene R. Bartlett claims that the active participation of the congregation while a sermon is being preached has not been taken seriously enough. . . . He calls on preachers to envision the worship in the pew as 'a subject acting, not an object acted upon.'"[1] In the 1980s, theologian Martin Marty asked, "Have you thought what a great part the people *may* play in weak or faulty preaching? What about the part people *must* play in preaching which works its fuller effect?" He admits, "I have been moved to learn something: the message has greatest effect when it is most clear that the people with whom I am a hearer are participating in preaching. They are 'preaching *with*.'"[2]

A commitment to "preaching *with*" begins before the sermon is preached—that is, in the preparation process, or, what is commonly called feedforward. I wholeheartedly agree with homiletician Tom Long, who has reminded us that "sermon preparation is not just preparation for ministry, it is ministry."[3] Why does this conviction matter? It affirms how important sermon preparation is. It honors the creative work of the preacher. It prioritizes the facilitation of creative and collaborative opportunities for people to gather around biblical stories that serve as the foundation for sermons.

Perhaps you are with me in theory but wondering what collaborative sermon preparation as a ministry looks like in practice. To be sure, there is no one right way to engage in this collaborative feedforward process.[4] Fred Craddock says one's feedforward process "will be most fruitful when it has become as comfortable as an old sweater."[5] Every old sweater is unique to its wearer. At some point, though, that sweater no longer fits or it wears out completely. In the same way, even our most tried-and-true processes need to be reformed. Imagine if the typewriter had never been challenged by companies working to develop a word processer. Imagine if we kept drilling at the same rate for petrol and did not support the emergence of electric vehicles. Imagine if we still did lobotomies to assist those with mental illness. In the same way, imagine if ordained clergy were still the only ones who could read the Bible, because they were the only ones who could read Latin, Hebrew, or Greek. Imagine if the standard practice was still simply to read from a body of sermons written by the church "fathers" who are centuries removed from our contemporary concerns and realities. Thank goodness for those who dare to don a new sweater when the occasion calls for it.

No feedforward process stays static over the life of one's preaching ministry. The preacher changes, learns new skills, and develops new relationships. No one feedforward process works for a preacher's changing context. While new preachers introduce new ways of doing ministry in a context, it is also true that the new preacher will be shaped by the context. Let's turn to a commonly overlooked part of the preparatory process—congregational exegesis.

Collaborative Congregational Exegesis

Homiletician James Nieman asserts, "We preach contextually, then, not merely because our preaching becomes more relevant but also so it more amply embodies a genuine encounter with Jesus."[6] For the sake of such genuine encounters, I encourage preachers to engage two levels of this contextual work in the congregation: broad and focused.

Broad

I suspect broad congregational exegesis is most intentionally engaged when one is first called to a new ministry setting. Common inquiries at this point include the following: What are the demographics of the people? The surrounding community? What is the history of the congregation? What is the congregation's vision for the future, and how do the people plan to get there? While ministers might think this exegetical work is a one-and-done task, Stephen Farris points out that is not true: "An exegesis of the situation is an unending or at least a frequently repeated task. It may be like painting the Golden Gate Bridge. By the time one has finished, it is time to start all over again."[7]

Preachers should make a plan to do such ongoing broad exegesis on a regular basis (perhaps once per year) in order to be attentive to the changing demographics of the neighborhood, to discover their congregation's everchanging theological leanings, and to understand how the church might respond faithfully in a potentially divisive political milieu.[8] Even more, preachers would do well to invite others to share in this process. Why? Because those of us called to preach have not earned the privilege to claim that the way we see the world is necessarily the way the world really is. Not only does "universalizing one's own experience" lead to ineffective communication, since doing so makes assumptions that might not be true, but it is potentially perilous to the gospel, since it often "characterize[s] only a segment, many times a dominant segment, of humanity," thereby further marginalizing those who are already "outside the norm."[9] The more preachers recognize their assumptions, the better: "Laying down our assumptions about our congregants may actually lead us to become more effective preachers."[10]

To assist in regularizing this "laying down of assumptions," preachers can connect congregational exegesis with their regular rhythms of sermon preparation. That practice is what I am referring to as "focused" congregational exegesis.

Focused

Other than prayer, which I am assuming is ever-present during every preacher's feedforward process, the first step for a preacher to craft a timely word is to reflect on the congregation's situation and situatedness in other contexts. Writing these reflections helps the sermon and serves as a helpful "record." Try it. As you consider your next occasion to preach, write two to three sentences for each of these prompts:

* What is happening in the world right now that will likely influence this sermon?
* What is happening in the church?
* What is happening in the congregation?
* What is happening in the lives of individual hearers?
* What is happening in your life?
* How might the liturgical season affect this sermon?

Remember to pray for these situations, specific events, and particular people as you move through the process.

This kind of contextual work is a profound spiritual practice and can be developed over time. It acknowledges that preachers engage the Bible not as blank slates but as socially located people who are deeply immersed in a variety of contexts just as their congregation members are. Attaching such articulation to each sermon makes for preaching that is "a timely word." Again, Nieman offers helpful insights: "We need not 'say it all' in a timelessly true yet assuredly remote sermon, but simply that the word is enough for today. It also imposes an obligation on every sermon to be attuned to what is happening now, since speaking to anything else would literally be a waste of time."[11]

Leander Keck encourages "priestly listening," in which the preacher listens to God's word on behalf of the congregation.[12] While Keck's encouragement is important, I am recommending that preachers go beyond this effort of listening on behalf of the congregation to actually listening to the congregation. Doing so acknowledges the limits of one's own social location. In other words, the preacher cannot possibly know what it is like to understand biblical stories from the points of view of the woman who always sits in the fifth pew with her Cheerios-eating children or the gay couple who sneaks into the back pew late and leaves early, perhaps for the sake of their anonymity. The contextual exegesis component of the feedforward process that is more collaborative embraces the recognition that our experiences are different from the next person's experiences—even experiences with biblical stories.

Numerous scholars have helped us understand that "every experience of a [biblical] text is particular to the interpreter and historically conditioned" and that no interpretation is "innocent" or "disinterred," to use Walter Brueggemann's terms: "Anyone who imagines that he or she is a benign or innocent preacher of the text is engaged in self-deception."[13] Elisabeth Schüssler Fiorenza denies "the existence of raw or uninterpreted experience" and warns preachers not to present their own experiences as though they are "paradigmatical for everyone."[14] Gardner Taylor admits, "The coloring and texturing of the sermon, no matter what the text may be, will be influenced by the personality and outlook of the preacher."[15] Rose asserts that the preacher's interpretation is most faithfully nuanced in conversation with other interpretations: "The exegetical task is not finished until the preacher knows the condition of the congregation and hears the text, as exegeted, speak to that condition. And the preacher should not guess at the condition of the people, any more than he or she should guess at the meaning of the text."[16]

It is neither helpful nor faithful to assume that what intrigues me in a biblical story is what moves the next person or to assume that what benefits me would necessarily benefit another person.

To recall that "Christ has made us 'fishers of [people]' (Mk 1:17) is to recall George Eliot's remark while listening to the complaints of some angling friends about the fruitlessness of their fishing: 'You should make a deeper study of the subjectivity of the trout.'"[17] In the interest of making a "deeper study of the subjectivity of the trout," preachers invite others to be conversation partners in the sermon-crafting process.

The more focused exegesis of the congregation—that is, the exegesis that works hand in hand with the weekly work of biblical exegesis—can be assisted by a common tool used by elementary school educators: the KWL chart.[18] The KWL chart is a process of discovery that identifies existing knowledge of a topic (what do you *k*now?), desired knowledge (what do you *w*ant to know?), and newfound knowledge (what did you *l*earn?). I add an additional step (*h*ow you will find out?). Thus we have a

KWHL chart. Here's how the KWHL chart works. As I think about the congregation and the upcoming sermon on Mark 2:1–8, for example, I would write in the K column of the chart what I *know* about the congregation that might shape how they hear this biblical story. For example, I know that some in this congregation have expressed uncertainty about Jesus's power to heal physical ailments. In this same row, but in the W column, I would write what I want to know about this claim. For example, I would want to know where this uncertainty comes from. Then in the H column, I would explore the possible ways to go about this inquiry. (The H column might include some of the practices this chapter describes below.) And then, finally, after collaborating with congregation members, I would write in the fourth column what I learned. This practice is an easy but effective way to connect congregational exegesis and biblical exegesis. (Chapter 7 explains the exercise in more detail and appendix B contains a completed sample and a blank chart for your use.)

Collaborative Biblical Exegesis

In order to move beyond the assumption that the way preachers interpret Scripture is normal and normative, preachers will want to invite "preaching partners" into the feedforward process. "Conversation partners" (or *homileo*-ing partners) in the sermon preparation process usually means colleagues (typically, other clergy) and scholars who have written commentaries. While these conversation partners are beneficial and important, consider whose voices are then privileged: ordained clergy, those who are highly educated, those who have been published, and typically, those with North American and European perspectives. Justo González and Catherine González propose that the word of God is best understood by the "powerless": "the Simon Peters of today's world—the fisherfolk on a lake in Nicaragua, the political prisoners in South Africa, the women whose rights are trampled."[19]

In addition to broadening the diversity of one's written "conversation" partners, I encourage preachers to broaden their verbal conversation partners to include their congregation members, who are their most important preaching partners. Such a partnership creates a community of interpreters that has the potential to increase the resonance between pulpit and pew and decrease the chances of the Bible becoming, as noted by the Gonzalezes, "an esoteric book that only those with specialized education or gifts can possibly be able to understand."[20]

Failure to democratize biblical interpretation unfaithfully legitimizes one perspective even though "no one person or group determines how others understand the Bible. No one controls the Bible or its meaning."[21]

Besides fusing focused congregational exegesis with biblical exegesis, another benefit to collaborative biblical exegesis is that when preachers listen deeply to the insights of their preaching partners, possible sermon content begins to emerge from and reflect the life of the congregation and its wider context. (Scouring the internet for poignant illustrations becomes unnecessary.) To be sure, preaching partners who have been a part of the feedforward process will listen differently—likely, more intently—to the sermon.

One might push against this proposal—"But I can't possibly ask everyone." Indeed. But not being able to reach everyone should not mean connecting with no one. It is OK to start small. Slowly but surely, a congregational culture that values preaching as a ministry of the whole congregation will emerge. Sermon preparation will become regularized congregational exegesis and create opportunities for relationship development and pastoral care as preachers find out more about who the people are, what energizes them, the grudges that keep them up at night, their unfilled life's dreams, and their understanding of who God is in their lives, for example. Even more, listeners getting to know their preachers and feeling empowered to enter the conversation may even lead to a better chance for the gospel to be heard. Now that sounds like ministry!

Some congregations already host a weekly Bible study based on the upcoming Sunday's lectionary readings. I wonder, though, what percentage of the time during that study the preacher speaks. Often Bible study means preachers sharing with congregation members what they know about the Bible, thereby reinforcing an elitism many homileticians have cautioned against. Other practices for Bible study are possible; some practices are new, and others require only slight tweaks during sermon preparation.

Don't "Reinvent the Wheel"

Preaching's transformative impact need not wait until the sermon is preached. Just as the preacher has been equipped to engage Scripture deeply, so too does the preacher equip preaching partners to do the same. Before equipping them with these skills, it is important for preachers to be aware of what they do and why.

Take a moment here to describe your process of engaging Scripture in sermon preparation. If you are not a preacher, ask your preachers if they would be willing to describe their process to you.

Perhaps your list includes some of these steps:

* Compare various biblical translations.
* Check the original language (Greek or Hebrew) of words that vary in the multiple translations.
* Explore the pericope in its larger context by asking (1) what comes immediately before and after the pericope and (2) what is significant about the pericope's placement in the entire book.
* Explore the history in and of the pericope.
* Explore the text through various lenses: theological or literary, for example.
* Read commentaries.[22]

Essentially, this list includes typical ways for engaging in historical-critical biblical interpretation. Now put an asterisk by those exercises that others do or could learn to do. While not every step has to be collaborative, it is worth considering which preparatory steps might become more communal.

Imagine the benefits of your congregation having a better sense of what you do when you study Sunday's lectionary texts. Then imagine the benefits of teaching them such skills for biblical exegesis. They're not meant to be a secret. Sure, you paid seminary tuition, but now you are remunerated, in part, to equip them! To use a contemporary pedagogical idiom, think of this possibility as a "flipped" Bible study. Rather than preachers telling others what they discovered after engaging these steps, they teach the steps and then invite others to share their discoveries with them.

Another small shift with a big impact is to consider thinking about the whole feedforward process as a spiritual practice. While some people engage in steps that feel more like a spiritual practice (e.g., *lectio divina*) than others, consider that each step has the potential to be, according to Elizabeth Liebert, "open to the action of the Spirit that comes to us as gift." Liebert says that to "have access" to the spiritual, "one must dispose oneself by means of practices (*askesis*, from which comes the word *exercise*, and carries the sense of bringing mastery via repetition)." She says, "A spiritual practice can be understood as the regular, repeated, intentional, embodied, actions that lead, step by step, toward enhanced good, true, and beautiful, shared with and evaluated within a community of shared practice according to agreed-upon standards of excellence."[23] Notice that Liebert challenges the notion that a spiritual practice is individualistic. She highlights the work of Rebecca Chopp in this regard. In *Saving Work*, "Rebecca Chopp notes that a practice is a 'socially shared form of behavior . . . a pattern of meaning and action that is both culturally constructed and individually instantiated. The notion of practice draws us to inquire into the shared activities of groups of persons that provide meaning and orientation to the world and that guide action.' Chopp, like others following Alasdair MacIntyre's treatment of *practice* in *After Virtue*, understands practices to be bodily, social, interactive, cooperative, and performed with rule-like regularities."[24] Even *oratio* (praying) can be understood at another level: "deep collegial sharing where each party engages as both initiator and receiver, listening together to how others see the same reality." Here Liebert engages quantum theorist David Bohm, who claims "this deep conversation, which he terms *dialogue*, furthers science, as it occurs when a group 'becomes open to the flow of a larger intelligence.' In this dialogue, participants seek to participate together in a larger pool of meaning that is always developing. In this kind of dialogue, the whole organizes the parts, and it can form individuals into a powerful learning community."[25]

Liebert's excitement for a possible "scholarly *oratio*" suggests that a whole sermon feedforward process might be considered *lectio divina* as people move together through (or perhaps in and out of) the *askesis* of *lectio* (reading), *meditatio* (ruminating), *oratio* (praying), and *contemplatio* (resting).

Rather than reinventing an entirely new process, engage the steps you already do in a new way—that is, as spiritual practices and as skills to be taught to others and as practices to be engaged with others.

Do Reform (!) Some Things

The steps listed above reflect what are classically understood to be a part of a historical-critical exegetical process. In addition to these valuable steps for biblical interpretation, I recommend developing feedforward practices that are more collaborative and more creative. Tom Long calls this part of the process "Attending to the Text" in which "we try to get to know the text in much the same way we would get to know a new friend, by spending time with [it], asking it many questions, and experiencing [it] in many different moods and contexts." We will "knock the barnacles off our assumptions about the text so that it can speak to us anew" as we engage in this "playful and freewheeling" part of the process.[26] He admits some far-fetched ideas could emerge from this kind of brainstorming. While such ideas will eventually be tested, biblical interpreters too often short-circuit this work in search of "the right interpretation." Long warns, "If we only perform the critical analysis and not the attentive listening, we will gather data *about* the Bible rather than hear the living word that comes *through* the Bible."[27]

Creative practices can be integrated into an existing Bible study, developed for a new Bible study, and/or facilitated in a piecemeal fashion throughout the week. The following recommended practices are not exhaustive but will get you started.[28] As you add more communal and creative practices to the feed-forward process, keep in mind some key points.

* Engage in a variety of practices in both face-to-face and web-conferencing environments. Some people had doubts that anyone would show up for a Bible study on Zoom. Those were the days! Now as I write this book in the middle of a global pandemic in which even Sunday morning worship is "virtually real" on Zoom, this notion does not sound so far-fetched.

* While you know best how your communities will respond to the invitation to participate, be open to surprise; people might be more willing than you imagine.

* Be patient. No practice is perfect on the first try.

* Remember that you are facilitating spaces to hear and learn from others, not to tell them what you know.

* Know that making these practices engaging, creative, and even fun is not sacrilegious; harnessing our creativity is reflective of a creative God who made us in that creative image.

* Introduce and facilitate practices that engage the whole person—mind, yes, and also emotions, imagination, and even the body! After all, the Shema in Deuteronomy 6:5 reminds us that we are called to love God not just with our minds but also with our hearts, our souls, and our

strength—indeed, our whole beings. Such kinesthetic and embodied learning brings to mind the Asaro Tribe of Indonesia and Papua New Guinea: "Knowledge is only a rumor until it lives in the muscle."

* Finally, again, make these practices collaborative. While there might be a time for one-on-one study/sharing, much of the power of this process is in your congregation members hearing the wisdom of one another.

The following practices have the potential to assist in equipping your communities to fulfill their baptismal calling to proclaim the gospel. To participate in them is to move beyond spending one's life watching others proclaim the gospel without ever having a safe and bold (!) space to practice doing it for oneself.

Creative and Collaborative Practices

The following collaborative and creative practices can be amended to suit the particularities of a context. Tweak them. Add to them. Some practices can be crowdsourced; that is, you announce an invitation for engagement on your website or Facebook. Others work best when you handpick participants. You decide.

Voice Recording of the Biblical Pericope

Now that most of us carry high-tech recording equipment wherever we go, it is easy to record the voices of others reading Sunday's gospel. Not only is this a hands-free way to hear the story multiple times while you are driving from the hospital to another meeting, but it affords you a peek into another's interpretations of a story by the way they read it. What an honor it would be to be invited by my pastor to accompany her throughout the week as she ruminates on God's living word. If your congregation is technically savvy, there could be a place on your website to access the recordings of anyone who wants to share their oral interpretation of the lectionary readings.

I Wonder / I Notice

No practice has received more "play" than this accessible and efficient, yet profound, way to let the biblical story speak. "I Wonder / I Notice" (IWIN—a serendipitous acronym!) invites listeners to speak while the biblical story is being read. They interrupt, yes, with statements that begin with either "I wonder" or "I notice." This practice was developed by the Godly Play Foundation, whose Montessori-based method provides a curriculum of spiritual practice that explores the mystery of God's presence in our lives. Reminiscent of Long's remark above, former archbishop of Canterbury Rowan Williams notes the directional shift that wondering promotes: "Spirituality is not so much an exercise of 'interrogating the data' of the Christian story and its traditions, but more importantly, the opportunity for the data to interrogate us (Williams, *The Wound of Knowledge*). Wondering ensures by its style (when carefully employed) that we are interrogated by the data—it asks questions of us, stimulates our authentic response and heightens an awareness of how it challenges us."[29] Let's take Mark 1:9–11 NIV as an example with IWIN statements inserted:

At that time [I wonder what time. I notice I better read what comes before this verse.] **Jesus came from Nazareth in Galilee and was baptized** [I wonder why Jesus, the Son of God, has to be baptized.] by John [I wonder if it is significant that it is John doing the baptizing.]

in the Jordan [I notice that place names seem important.]. **Just as Jesus was coming up out of the water** [I notice his was probably a full-immersion baptism.] **he saw heaven being torn open** [I wonder if Jesus was scared. I wonder if anyone else was there and noticed the same thing. I notice it does not say that even John noticed the heavens being torn open.] **and the Spirit descending** [I wonder if it was a slow descent or if this too could have been frightening.] **on him like a dove.** [I wonder why a dove.] **And a voice came from heaven** [I notice this is the second "thing" to come from the heavens being torn open. I wonder if the voice always follows the Spirit. Again, I wonder if anyone else heard the voice.]: **"You are my Son, whom I love; with you I am well pleased."** [I wonder how Jesus felt when he heard these words. I wonder if I heard that voice at my baptism.]

It might take a couple of fits and starts for reticent people to jump in, but it never takes long before people are thoughtfully and often joyfully wondering aloud. There is no pressure to answer all of these questions; we are released from having to have all the right answers. In fact, at this point we will not have any answers at all. We are freed to respect all responses as our brainstorming functions to "let it all out." This kind of playfulness "supports getting into an 'alternative reality' mindset, that throws open possibilities and frees up defences, and thus inspires a quality of intrepid spiritual exploration not just clever thinking."[30]

What a wonder-filled way to begin a council meeting or a Bible study. The practice requires us to slow down and really

87

let the details of those stories—even those we think we know so well—come alive. The communal nature is significant for it immediately points to the power of collective inquiry. Compare this practice with simply reading the story, often very quickly, and then opening the Bible study by asking, "So what do you think this means?" The latter promotes jumping to conclusions rather than engaging.

After engaging in this practice, be sure to debrief the experience. While some might express frustration at the seeming chaos of people speaking all at once and not providing answers, most will be delighted by being liberated from the restraints of having to be "good children" who quietly listen and dare not question the sacred word of God. Inevitably, someone affirms how wonderful it is to hear what others wonder and notice.

Scripture Tableau

In a Scripture tableau, people present an embodied depiction of a biblical story by physically offering still/"frozen" poses.[31] Other than IWIN, I have found that this practice yields some of the most profound engagement with a biblical story in ways that surprise even the most reluctant participants. The practice does not require professional actors, props, or fancy sets. It is beloved by adults and young people alike, and it works with small or large groups. (If you've got a large group, you can send small groups to separate rooms and then compare the results at the end. The experience is like comparing biblical translations but with live, human bodies.)

Planning is required for this activity. First, I do some exegetical (contextual, historical, and lexical) work ahead of time so that, if need be, I can gently steer people from getting too far from the details of the story. As much as possible, though, letting people explore interpretive possibilities is most beneficial. Often others in the group steer one another back to the details of the story. Next, I remove verse numbers, which distract from the story's movement, in order to divide the story into scenes. Note that we are not changing any biblical words or their order, just chunking them into scenes. Here is an example of the first few scenes from Mark 2:1–8 NIV:

> **Scene 1:** A few days later, when Jesus again entered Capernaum, the people heard that he had come home. They gathered in such large numbers that there was no room left, not even outside the door, and he preached the word to them.
>
> **Scene 2:** Some men came, bringing to him a paralyzed man, carried by four of them. Since they could not get him to Jesus because of the crowd, they made an opening in the roof above Jesus by digging through it and then lowered the mat the man was lying on.
>
> **Scene 3:** When Jesus saw their faith, he said to the paralyzed man, "Son, your sins are forgiven."

Each participant has a printed copy of the scenes in hand. I make it clear to all participants that this division is only temporary, since we might learn something about how to divide the scenes by actually engaging in the activity itself.

At the beginning of the "rehearsal" (which is itself the Bible study), we read the story and list the characters. I ask for volunteers to play each character. Even that is instructive. Who is reticent to play Jesus? Why? Who is quick to play Jesus? Why? Indeed, embodying the characters leads to profound empathic experiences for the players. Even the shyest Bible study attendees tend to participate with questions or suggestions or, at least, by describing what they see in the poses. This practice yields a long list of questions for the preacher to explore and may even offer a few possible "leads" for the sermon.

If the players are willing, the tableau can be presented during the reading of the gospel in worship. As each scene is read, the congregation closes their eyes while the "players" get into their poses. When the congregation is invited to open their eyes, they have five seconds or so to see the embodied interpretation before them before being invited to close their eyes again while the reading continues and the "players" get into their next poses. If I do use a tableau in worship, I will ask the players to meet again after I've done more work with the biblical text. I may even ask the players to adjust their poses so that they resonate with the direction of the sermon (much in the same way I might modify the emphasis, cadence, and eye contact, for example, during the reading of the gospel in order to align with the sermon).

I recall a student offering to play the role of the paralytic when we were "staging" Mark 2:1–8. "Theresa" was a very bright student and also very respected by her peers. She was a lively participant in class and tended to have very good insights. However, as the paralyzed person in the story, imagine what her experience was like for the forty-five minutes of the study as the voiceless one who only had the capacity to lie on the mat and receive the help of those around her.

We were all moved by Theresa's reflections shared during the debrief of our experience. She was so humbled by the experience of being totally dependent on others and realized that she had lived her life as a very privileged person—as one who is able-bodied and generally empowered to speak. Theresa had a new-found sense of dependence on Jesus and interdependence with her community. When we presented this tableau in worship during the reading of the gospel, the final scene had an impact on the whole congregation. Their eyes were closed when the gospeler read: "'But so that you may know that the Son of Man has authority on earth to forgive sins,' he said to the paralytic, 'I say to you, stand up, take your mat and go to your home.' And he stood up, and immediately took the mat and went out before all of them; so that they were all amazed and glorified God, saying, 'We have never seen anything like this!'" When the congregation opened their eyes expecting to see new poses in the chancel, they had to turn their heads to the aisle where Theresa was standing, holding her mat, with exuberant joy on her face having been restored both physically and socially; she was re-membered into the community by her health. The tableau preached, and as the one listed in the bulletin as the preacher, I only accompanied its proclamation.

"Scripture tableau" powerfully emulates the work of the Brazilian theatre visionary and Nobel Peace Prize–winner Augusto Boal (1931–2009). His community-based Theatre of the Oppressed, which uses theatre as a tool for social change, reminds me also of various works on embodied learning—kinesthetics. Kinesthesia, Pamela Ann Moeller notes, "does not mean just movement—kinetics—but movement *and* the sensory experience and memory that result from movement and . . . generate new movement."[32] A new movement was generated on that day in worship when Theresa's willingness to embody the paralytic propelled us into the world with a new empathy for one another, compassion for ourselves, and gratefulness for Jesus's power to heal.

Literary Exercise

Another way to encourage a close reading of the experiences of the characters in the story is to invite participants to describe the events in the story from the perspective of one of the characters (thus a first-person singular point of view). Only three to five minutes of freewriting can yield creative and enlightening results. People then share what they've written in small groups. With permission from the creator, these stories can serve as an illustration in the sermon.

Photography Exercise

Just as nearly everyone has a voice recorder on their phones, nearly everyone is always carrying a camera. Invite people to submit photographs they take throughout the week that respond to a prompt related to the biblical story. For example, where do you see indifference to "the least of these"? Where is there evidence of taking to heart (and to the streets) Jesus's Sermon on the Mount? Instead of "Made in the USA," show us through your photography "Made in the Image of God." The photographers' submissions will inspire your sermon preparation. Inviting them to write a bit about why they took the shot as they did in light of the biblical story goes to the next level of engagement. Whether or not you utilize the photographs during the sermon, they can play on a loop as people enter the sanctuary (or Zoom).

Musical Exercise

Invite people to describe how they would orchestrate a certain biblical story. What would be the time signature of the story of Jesus's baptism noted above? What key would it be in and why? Would there be any key changes? Which instruments would be highlighted when and why? For example, what sound best depicts the tearing of the heavens? The dove descending? The voice from heaven? Just the imaginative exercise offers insight into how the story is impacting their lives and is a much more interesting way to engage than simply responding to "What do you think this text means?"

Additional Exercises

Another way to invite participation is to tap into your people's vocations and avocations. For example,

1. Ask the educators in your congregation and community to offer practices they use to help students engage stories.
2. Invite those whose work is in theatre or film actors to help stage the scene.
3. Ask your congregation's visual artists to depict scenes using a medium of their choice.
4. Empower your community's songwriters, spoken word artists, and poets to create pieces that reflect their engagement with a biblical story.

Even if nothing concrete finds its way into the sermon itself, the process is not ineffective. You've engaged in Bible study together. You've held space for people to speak and listen to one another. You've found out a bit more about one another's lives. In doing these things, you've invited others into the preaching ministry of the congregation. Along the way, you might even feel inclined to nudge toward seminary or, at least, toward preaching every once in a while.

"Test" the Sermon's Possible Impact

As preachers put words to paper, they can test certain sections with some listeners, carefully observing whether and how impact matches intent. While practicing the sermon aloud is an important by-product of this step, the main benefit is to listen to how others hear the sermon draft. For example, a preacher might think he is affirming all people and their circumstances by saying, "It doesn't matter if you are Black or white, rich or poor, male or female, gay or straight, you are welcome here." And yet when "rehearsing" the delivery of the sermon (or part of a sermon) in front of another, the preacher discovers the impact of the words is hurtful; that is, they suggest that the particularities of my lived experience don't matter. Even more, they reinforce simplistic and unhelpful binaries. Upon learning that the impact does not mirror one's good intentions, the preacher can adjust accordingly. Note that this is not a matter of simply giving people what they want to hear but rather hearing what is heard so that the proclamation can most effectively announce good news.

I imagine this kind of "testing" to be especially helpful when the preacher plans to address a social issue that is divisive or might cause some to say, "Politics do not belong in the pulpit." I am writing this chapter in the days after a violent mob attacked the US Capitol (January 6, 2021). Preachers are compelled to respond to these events in their sermons on Sunday, January 10. For those congregations that have already established a culture of collaboration and conversation connected to their preaching ministry, it will be easier to gather together and explore effective and faithful ways to address concerns from the pulpit.[33]

Use whatever resources are helpful to craft biblically grounded, theologically astute, pastorally present sermons, including literature, film, podcasts, art, poetry, and the newspaper. And, very importantly, don't forget the most important resources of all—the people. Why rely on another's curated content for illustrations when life is happening before your very eyes? *Collaborative and creative feedforward* exercises make a difference for a congregation's preaching ministry and for ministry, in general. Every student in every preaching class I facilitate has had to do this. They've discovered that their assumptions that congregation members don't have time for or a desire to engage in creative and collaborative biblical exegesis with them often have been wrong. Congregants yearn to engage in such processes. People feel a hunger they are sometimes not even aware of until they are fed. We turn now to the difference feedforward groups can make during preaching.

For Reflection and Discussion

1. Describe ways your congregation already engages in Bible study together. To what extent is this Bible study a part of the preaching ministry of the congregation?
2. Which of the proposed practices are you interested in trying and why?
3. What other creative and collaborative practices (or amendments to the options above) would you like to try and why?
4. In what way(s) do you think preachers inviting listeners to be a "sounding board" for a portion of the sermon could make a positive impact on a preaching ministry?

5

Feed
Stewarding the Pulpit

Exploring the context and Scripture with a variety of conversation partners shapes both the content (what is said) and the form (how it is said) of sermons. The sermon feedforward process proposed in this book yields illustrations, stories, and perspectives from the congregation that might appear in the sermon. While the primary speaker is still typically called the minister, other individuals might have brief cameos in the sermon itself. Each preaching context will need leaders to negotiate what is possible and what pushes boundaries too far. In every case, the goal is to "get the gospel heard." But like a ship whose direction changes significantly with the slightest turn, so, too, small adjustments in the preaching process will have great effect down the way.

Overall, I recommend avoiding the two extremes of (1) the Lone-Ranger preacher who takes sole charge for crafting and preaching the sermon[1] and (2) an open-ended time of "sharing," such as a twenty-minute "open mic" session in the middle of worship or an "ask me anything" Q&A between preacher and

congregation.[2] Possibilities for broader congregational participation, what I am calling "embodied participation," during the
sermon explored in this chapter include shifting the sermon's
trajectory, tapping into the gifts of others, and evoking the community's voice (different from an open-ended Q&A). HyeRan
Kim-Cragg affirms the importance of these possibilities in her
important book *Postcolonial Preaching*: "Just as preaching should
not be understood exclusively in terms of a verbal exercise, neither should it be understood as a solo endeavor. An appreciation
of the role of the preacher as shared and owned by the whole
community is essential. Preaching has no weight unless it is the
corporate body of faith that lives by it. . . . Preaching as a theological body language uses the language of social relationships
that is formed by the community."[3] A final possibility explored
in this chapter is to broaden representation of those whose bodies are seen and heard in worship. But first, perhaps the most
common difference a communal feedforward process makes is a
shift in the trajectory of the sermon content.

Shift the Sermon's Trajectory

A student was facilitating our Bible study on the story of the
"Bold Samaritan" (yes, *bold*—the titling of the parable made all
the difference for her). She invited her preaching partners to free-
write from the perspective of one of the characters in the story
(the "literary exercise" proposed in the previous chapter). In just
five minutes, the group produced creative perspectives from the
first-person point of view. The result was a newfound connection with one of the characters—in the student's words, "the
guy lying on the road." Once the group "began to really see this
person," momentum picked up for a possible sermon trajectory.

The preacher decided not to exhort hearers to help those in need, since, while not an unfaithful possibility, it was the only trajectory any of the partners had ever heard. Instead, the primary direction of the sermon was from the perspective of one whose need was ignored.

Another example comes from someone who was working on a sermon based on Mark 1. Many things happen in quick succession in that pericope, but the preacher anticipated the congregation would appreciate a focus on Jesus's baptism and, by extension, the importance of their church's practice of baptism. What she discovered from engaging in the creative and collaborative exercises ahead of time, however, was that her partners were most energized, intrigued, and even inspired by Jesus's time in the wilderness. She knew she had to shift the trajectory for that particular sermon given the wilderness-like context her partners were experiencing.

Congregation members offer so much to preachers. In addition to welcoming congregation members' perspectives, preachers would do well to tap into their gifts.

Tap into the Gifts of Others

Preachers know that congregation members are not blank slates, but they often forget to tap their wisdom, expertise, and experience for biblical understanding and even sermon content. Unfortunately, more often preachers turn to the internet for illustrations, even though it is very unlikely that such illustrations will strengthen relationships. Why not connect with those farmers in the congregation when the parable of the sower appears in the lectionary? Consider inviting those first responders and health care workers to a conversation around the healing stories in Scripture. Tap their experienced wisdom. Let them know you need their partnership to preach on these stories. (Of course, should you utilize that wisdom, remember to ask for permission to share it and to acknowledge the source.)

I recommend going one step further and inviting those experts to speak at a fitting moment in the sermon. While some people might not wish to speak, being invited to do so honors their voices. When someone is willing to do so, the results can be powerful.

James Aalgaard, pastor of Grace Lutheran Church in Wenatchee, Washington, remembers vividly one of his seminary intern's "live" sermon illustrations. In an Advent sermon, Jenna Bergeson explored the sentence from Scripture, "There shall come forth a shoot from the stump of Jesse, and a branch from his roots shall bear fruit":[4] "So from a great tree, we get a stump. And from that stump, a shoot shall grow. As you know, I'm not from this area but I've heard there's a lot of tree growing that happens around here. Am I right? Well, I'm wondering: how legit is this whole idea of a shoot growing out of stump? There must be someone here who knows. Tory Schmidt, you know about tree-growing, right?" At this point, Bergeson invites Schmidt, a member of the congregation who is a pear grower and a scientist and researcher for the fruit-tree industry, to join her in front and asks him to explain how shoots grow out of stumps. With a back-and-forth interview style, Bergeson draws out Schmidt's wisdom on grafting for orchard renewal. Finally, she asks, "What is the best way to bear fruit?" Schmidt responds, "In some respects, the focus on fruit becomes a bit of a distraction for growers. As a plant physiologist, I like to think about what makes the tree happy. In many respects, what I encourage our growers to think about is, we're not growing fruit; we're essentially farming light. And so we want to do everything we can to set our trees up to optimize so that they have the best chance to capture as much sunlight as possible, and then fruit becomes a by-product of that, one of the side benefits of keeping your tree happy." Bergeson thanks Schmidt and the congregation claps as he makes his way back to his seat. That last question and response launch the sermon into a reflection on a recent baptism:

> The focus is capturing light. And bearing good fruits is a result of capturing that light. Wow. A few weeks ago, we had a baptism and welcomed Greyson into our family, another branch on this family tree that started with a shoot from a stump. I believe that through our baptism, we are all rooted in Christ, ultimately bound and connected to each other and to God's unwavering love for us. But it's also part of our duty and our delight to seek out the light of God . . . through worship, in prayer, and in service as God's hands and feet in this world. We have good days and we have bad days doing that, but when we seek and capture/harvest the light of God, it becomes part of our nature to bear good fruits.

A playful tone imbues this section of the sermon without being "corny" or "schmaltzy." Sharing the mic in no way minimizes the sacredness of the pulpit. I am inclined to say that the communal engagement actually heightens the sacredness of preaching.

Mary Lou Baumgartner was a pastor in Ohio when she tapped into the experience of a community member:

> When I was serving a central city parish in Toledo, Ohio, I was blessed to serve with Tony, a neighbor who

had first come to our Tuesday evening community meal when he heard that we served good food. He came back because he heard the good news—that he was loved by God! His favorite verse was Ephesians 2:8: "For by grace you have been saved through faith, and this is not your own doing; it is the gift of God." Tony had wandered far from the faith of his youth, and when he experienced being beloved of God, he grasped the grace that had saved him; he knew that it was not by his effort but only by God's grace that he had been saved. He was always happy to tell others who came to church—whether for food or good news—about God's grace and mercy.

When I was searching for an example of someone whose life witnessed to God's saving grace . . . , I realized that there was no better example than Tony. I asked him if he'd join me in preaching that week, to tell his story and to share his favorite verse. I set up the text and then invited him forward. When he finished his story, I concluded the sermon. His witness to Jesus was far more powerful than any illustration I could have researched or written. Tony was my illustration.[5]

No internet illustration could strengthen a relationship like this living illustration did.

Each of these preachers utilized the "prophetic proclamation" strategy Leonora Tubbs Tisdale calls "inviting someone personally involved in the concern to participate in preaching on it."[6] Tisdale offers an example: "What if the pastor, whose college-student congregant had spent her spring break engaged in a protest at the School for the Americas in Americus, Georgia, and who had been arrested for her civil disobedience there, invited the parishioner to tell her story as a part of the Sunday sermon and then spent the rest of the sermon reflecting on the nature of Christian civil disobedience and its long history in the life of our nation and world?"[7]

Tisdale asserts that pastors are "not only crafting theology for their parishioners; they are also modeling for them how to become local theologians themselves" as they bring "the Bible and theology and life experiences together in an integrative, fitting, and transformative way."[8] Preachers underutilize "sharing the mic" in this way despite its impact.

Building on the concept of literally passing the microphone to (or sharing with) one other person in the sermon, the gathered body might also be invited to speak during the sermon.

Evoke the Community's Voice

"Call and response" between preacher and congregation is typical in some communities and unprecedented in others. Coaxing (not forcing) the collective voice in the midst of the sermon can be one way for people to gain "competence and confidence" in using their own voices to proclaim the gospel. James Aalgaard does this in his sermon based on Mark 4:35–41.[9]

As Aalgaard reads the gospel, multiple voices join him in saying Jesus's words, "Peace, be still." This vocalization by others in addition to the preacher foreshadows the last three minutes of the sermon, when Aalgaard transitions from the disciples' experience during the storm to the storms present in the lives of those in his congregation:

> In our storms, we might think Jesus is asleep, uncaring.
> But really, he's exercising absolute faith. And he's ready

with a word. Here are some possible winds of worry going on in our hearts, dear people of Grace:

* I'm concerned about getting along with my room-mates when I'm in Houston. Peace, be still.
* When I serve out in the communities of the city during the Youth Gathering, I'm worried about seeing something that makes me feel uncomfortable. Peace, be still.
* I don't know what it will be like interviewing for my first call in a congregation, and I hope I can get a sense of God's will and direction. Peace, be still.

In this third statement, already members' voices of the congregation can be heard joining in, "Peace, be still."

* My spouse recently died, and I don't like eating alone, and my bed is too big for just me. Peace, be still.
* My grandkids seem to have left the church, maybe even the Christian faith altogether. Peace, be still.

By this point, the preacher stops speaking and yields to the congregation's collective voice, "Peace, be still." They are gracing one another.

* My congregation has begun conversations about our welcome of people of all sexual and gender identities, and I don't know how comfortable I'll be. Peace, be still.

* I want to be in worship, but I'm not a very social person. Peace, be still.

These examples come directly from the community's expressed concerns. Finally, the preacher affirms, "We could come up with so many more, right? Dear family of Grace, he is still speaking peace. His voice sounds a lot like yours. Peace, be still. Peace, be still. The storm rages; peace, be still." With one voice, their own voices, members of the congregation minister to one another.

Sometimes the voices of those in the congregation change the direction of the sermon in the midst of preaching, prompting the preacher to go "off script." One of the most famous examples did not take place in a worship setting, per se. But it did indeed propel the speaker to start preaching. Rev. Dr. Martin Luther King Jr. was delivering a speech on civil rights in Washington, DC, on August 28, 1963, when Mahalia Jackson cajoled him, "Tell them about the dream, Martin." Writer ZamaMdoda recounts the moment:

> This time, it wasn't an aide or King's advisor and speechwriter Clarence Jones that nudged the dial towards history-making—it was gospel singer Mahalia Jackson. From 50 feet away, in the middle of the biggest speech of King's career, Jackson called on Martin Luther King Jr., the preacher with her words "Tell them about the dream, Martin! Tell them about the dream!"
>
> Jones . . . recounted the moment as "one of the world's greatest gospel singers shouting out to one of the world's greatest Baptist preachers." It was a call to action disguised in the smooth warmth of your auntie's

"Go on, baby." King answered that call to one of the greatest Jazz singers of his age—a woman who would accompany him on the most trying parts of his journey. . . .

It took a Black woman to remind the politician that only the preacher could give this sermon and the fact that we are still speaking about it means the world needed to hear it and still does. That being the case, the speech and Jackson's call to remember "the dream" reveal that dreaming can be solitary, right up until a Black woman is involved.[10]

King's willingness to be influenced by others is a model for leadership for us all. A blogger on *A Pastor's Workshop* also reflects on this occasion: "I love this little insight into one of the most important moments in American history, not because it lessens King's impact and genius, but rather, enlarges it. It also speaks to the genius and boldness of Mahalia Jackson, willing, in one of the biggest moments of her life and Dr. King's, to speak up with a great idea. How wonderful for King not to scoff or ignore her, but to listen, pause and realize that she was right, that now it was time to tell them about the dream."[11]

Perhaps preachers are so mired in their expectation to influence others that they forget to be open to the influence of others. Researcher and writer Brené Brown reminds us that a sign of emotional maturity for those in leadership positions is being influenced by others. Thankfully, the church's efforts to propel us into a new way have paid off. One of these efforts, as noted in chapter 3, is the recognition that earlier missionary efforts were oppressive. That is, the missionary-as-actor whose work it was to influence another, the "acted-upon," missed the essential component of mutuality. Again, as noted in chapter 3, an accompaniment model of mission work recognizes that all parties involved are open to influencing and being influenced.

Another effort is in fact related to preaching—and not so new. In the late 1960s, homiletician Reuel Howe was lamenting monological preaching in which "the laity has been assigned the role of passive consumer rather than active participant."[12] Howe insisted the principles of dialogue should be adhered to in preaching, particularly the principle that calls for participants to be open to one another: "If communication is two-way, then preaching should mean communication: (1) between congregation and preacher; and (2) between members of the congregation and people with whom they live and work. All of this transaction is part of the total act of preaching and has an important bearing upon our understanding of what a sermon is."[13]

Prompting the community to let their voices be heard during the sermon is one way to honor the mutual influence of preacher and listener. But why stop with just the voice? Embodied participation of the gathered community has potential to expand the influence of the priesthood of all believers.

I am hoping our preaching ministries reflect the newer accompaniment model of mission, engage Scripture contrapuntally, and adhere to principles of dialogue so that we do not simply formulate what we'll say next but really listen and be open to the influence of the other.[14]

Encourage Embodied Participation

What do people do with their bodies during worship? They sit and stand in one's chosen or assigned space. They shake hands with or hug one another during the passing of the peace. They walk up to the altar to receive holy communion and then walk back to the pew. These actions are embodied participation. Now what about during the sermon? What do people do with their bodies during the sermon? I suspect many of us will respond with a simple, "Sit still." Of course, not all of us would answer in this way. Take, for example, homiletician Teresa Fry Brown's description of the active role of the listener in accepting or rejecting the sermon: "It is important to remember that call and response in the black church setting may be verbal, nonverbal, or both. People may wave a hand, clap, stand up, run, cry, shake their heads, rock back and forth, moan, hum, kneel, or even throw items at the preacher in an affirming sort of way."[15]

For those of us who answered "sit still" above, I suspect it would not be too uncommon for the one person to be moving during the sermon to be the preacher. She is probably standing instead of sitting. She gestures occasionally. Sometimes she might wander back and forth in front of the church.

Why is it usually just the preacher's body that is engaged in a variety of ways during the sermon when we know how effective embodied participation is for learning and staying engaged? When asked how they learn best, most people do not say, "By hearing." (However, the number of podcasts and audio books suggests to me that hearing is still an effective way to be engaged.[16]) Many people say they are visual learners. Most people say that they learn by doing. Our educational systems have listened to this latter claim, recognized the reasons behind it, and adjusted accordingly. They have embraced more embodied pedagogies, more opportunities to "learn by doing" (no small thanks is due to the work of John Dewey in the late nineteenth and early twentieth centuries). Listening to the teacher describe a chemistry experiment is far less effective than mixing hydrogen peroxide and potassium iodide.

Only the latter requires safety goggles, a sure sign of participation. Golfers do not get a hole in one solely by thinking about their swing. Mindfulness is important, but eventually, a person must pick up the club. Actually setting fingers to a keyboard is a good idea before performing at the piano recital. And yet our congregation members primarily learn about the Bible by sitting still in the pews and listening to one other person speak for twelve to twenty minutes. In homiletics—the discipline of reflecting on preaching practices—we've even accepted calling those in the *audience* "hearers" or "listeners," the latter assuming a more active stance.

We've made some adjustments along the way, adjustments that recognize humans' kinesthetic intelligence. In the interest of living into the claim that the liturgy is understood to be "the work of the people," we've sought ways to involve everyone in worship. Even sanctuary design has changed to reflect a desire for more involvement of everything (e.g., "church in the round," movable pews/chairs).

We've even made adjustments during the sermon. The story above is one such example. The physical shift of Schmidt as he made his way to the pulpit symbolizes a connection between pulpit and pew. A similar connection is signified when the preacher moves from a high, faraway pulpit into the midst of the people. Also, preachers are aware of how posture, gestures, and facial expressions create meaning.

All of these adjustments acknowledge the difference it makes when the body gets involved in some way in the proclamation of the word. While these shifts alone make a major difference in a congregation's preaching ministry, this section goes one step further. Because, again, focusing only on the preacher's movements during the sermon falls short of the call of all of us, not just the ordained pastor, to love God with our whole beings (Deut 6). Of course, yes, we do this in other parts of our lives. But why not get our whole bodies involved during the sermon? It is time to embrace a homiletic that recognizes how the body—our individual bodies and our collective being as the body of Christ—remembers. The body re-members; that is, it rejoins each in the community one to another.

Seminary professor and pastor Pamela Ann Moeller recalls when the importance of utilizing the whole body in preaching clicked for her: "After years of training my mind toward coherent, articulate theological thinking and expression, I discovered that my body was also a voice, a voice without words, but one that is capable of expression quite beyond the abilities of my mind and mouth."[17] Moeller's book *A Kinesthetic Homiletic*, focuses on kinesthetics, the "sensory experience and memory that result from movement." She argues that "we are long overdue in bringing theology and physicality, thought, movement and its sensory memory, sermons, and gospel embodiments together intentionally honoring them as a coherent whole."[18]

People know "in their bones" the importance of the whole body and may need just a nudge to unlearn the Enlightenment-era prioritization of "mind over matter." After guiding congregation members through the Scripture tableau exercise in a Bible study, one preacher shared that the participants themselves noted that they felt like they truly embodied the Word. One parishioner's profound discovery, "I had to be the Word rather than read it," affirms HyeRan Kim-Cragg's encouragement that "preachers should get in touch with their bodies in the process of preparing to preach, and congregations should be invited to exercise their own bodies in the course of the worship event as a way of harnessing the communicative power of the Incarnate

Word."[19] What follows are examples of this kind of "getting in touch with" and "exercising" our bodies when preparing to preach and when preaching.

One of the creative and collaborative exercises that prompts people to "be the Word" is the "Scripture tableau" explained in a previous chapter. Mark Holmerud, former bishop of the Sierra Pacific Synod of the Evangelical Lutheran Church in America (ELCA), not only utilized the exercise as sermon preparation, but he also made it part of the sermon itself:

> Three tableaus were conceived and presented by three different groups of [conference] participants—each one with a different way of telling the story. I was to pick one as the way the Gospel would be shared later that evening. In the first two tableaus, Lazarus was depicted as lying in the tomb, but in the third tableau, Lazarus, appearing to be wrapped in burial cloths, was standing, "front and center," throughout the three "poses" that were offered.
>
> The final pose of this tableau was Lazarus emerging from the tomb, and people's reactions to that moment. Lazarus, standing in the middle of that tableau, demonstrated to me a part of the story we must attend to, in that each of us, in the moment of responding to the death of a friend or loved one in our own life, cannot forget the ways that person has been so present in our lives. I (and Spirit, to whom I give 100 percent "credit" for what comes next) made the choice to ask those who were in the tableau to remain in their last pose as I began the sermon. I then began to wander through the tableau, sharing a reflection on the reaction of each person

or group of people to the moment of Lazarus emerging from the tomb. I would stand near them, and then gently touch them on the shoulder so they could "leave" the tableau as I moved on to the next person or group. I spent a few moments speaking about these people—the grief and then joy of Mary and Martha, the murderous rage of the scribes, bystanders who were moved by Jesus' tears, and Jesus, aware of the cost of this moment to his earthly journey. I ended my sermon by standing next to Lazarus and wondering about his "getting" to die twice as a result of his being raised, and yet how we are called to die each day to our sin and selfishness, and then to rise in the grace and memory of our baptism to live for others.

In my prayer time preparing to preach that night, I came to think of Scripture tableaus as reminding me of walking through memorial gardens—the Dr. Martin Luther King Jr. Memorial . . . or the Holocaust Memorial in Berlin, or in cemeteries where we seek out the markers of lost loved ones. Each of these sacred places is "pause-worthy." If we hurry through them, we might miss a moment of inspiration, challenge, grace, or peace.[20]

The impact of such embodiment of God's word lingers for those who are the players in the scene, other congregation members, and preachers too.

I, too, have experimented with use of the Scripture tableau during a sermon based on the story in Mark 1 about Jesus's invitation for the fisherman to follow him. With the agreement of the tableau players, I invited them back up to the front of the sanctuary midway through the sermon. At that point, I invited anyone in the congregation to come forward and "tap out" one of the players in order to offer their own pose and expression, depending upon how they think that particular character would react. I modeled this practice after Augusto Boal's work with "spect-actors" in Theatre of the Oppressed (see chapter 3). Lo and behold, four or five different people who had not participated in the Bible study earlier in the week boldly moved from being spectators to spect-actors. I came to understand later that this sermon move was one of the most memorable. I suspect that is so because (1) people were invited to participate in a way that asked them to use their bodies and (2) their insights and offerings were respectfully treated.

As impactful as the Scripture tableau can be, especially if it is then presented during the gospel reading in worship (and then utilized during the sermon), it does take time and energy to work with it. Embodying the word need not be this intense if time does not allow. Three examples illustrate this point.

In the feedforward Bible study for a sermon I was to preach based on Psalm 63, someone asked, "What does it look like for me to bless God? Isn't God the one who blesses me?" He was referring to verse 4, when the Psalmist declares, "So I will bless you as long as I live." I had not thought of his question in my preparatory work. The insightful discussion that ensued led to our sharing with one another what blessing looks like . . . using our bodies. This kinesthetic prompt shaped the sermon. (Note that I was a guest preacher and let the pastor know ahead of time what I had been planning to do. Since she had warned me how unusual the "ask" would be, I tried to playfully nudge the congregation to participate.) Here is an excerpt of the sermon:[21]

I wonder how one blesses God. How do <u>you</u> bless God?

Let me ask you this: if you were the subject of a photograph and wanted to symbolize "blessing," what would you do? <u>Think on that for a moment.</u> Someone is taking a picture of you, and you want the viewers to understand that you are blessing, what would you do?

Now I realize I'm a guest, so this is a bit daring, but I am going to ask you to strike that pose. Think of it as a kind of **liturgical charades.**

So it's a still photograph, but feel free to use all of the space around you in order to strike your pose. Are you ready?

I already know you are never going to invite me back, right? You think it's **risky** to do this, I know; you might like silly. Imagine how risky it is for me. **My profound (wink!) point depends on your participation.**

So for those who are willing, are you ready to strike that pose? I will do this too, on the count of three: 1 . . . 2 . . . 3.

Let's give it another shot. Now that you have seen some possibilities, others can join in: 1 . . . 2 . . . 3.

Without breaking your pose too much, look around. What do you see?

Let me tell you what I notice: Some are standing, some sitting, some kneeling, arms raised, hands placed on an imaginary being, mouths open.

Right now, and here's that important point, I hope you think it's profound—it's not mine, it's the Psalmist's: **you are blessing with your soul.**

This use of the whole body, at least more of our bodies than we typically use, became the foundation to engage a problematic body/soul split, which then led to an encouragement to reconsider how we understand "soul." The idea was to encourage people to use the whole body, one's whole being, to praise God. The embodied still photographs from the beginning would be activated in the world:

> Remember those still photographs you made and imagine they have a little sideways triangle on them and, with our mouse, you left-click on it.
> Voilà . . . movement . . . sound.
> Now there is an added level of blessing the Lord with what is a blessing from the Lord. . . .
> For those of you who have ever wondered why in worship we sit, stand, kneel, speak, sing, eat, drink, et cetera. This is why: we are engaging our souls in praising God.

> At the end of the day, our wholeness—the wellness of our souls—isn't ours because we received our certificate of completion in spiritual direction boot camp.
> Rather, the wellness of our souls is ours because of God's steadfast love.

> People of the incarnation, from this time forward the "play" triangle is pressed and you are invited to praise God as the Psalmist did:
> Your mouths open,

> singing for joy with your bodies upright,
> and your souls clinging to the right hand
> that upholds you.

Had I thought of it at the time, I would have asked people to strike their blessings poses once again at the time of the benediction. Then I would invite someone from the congregation to come forward and mimic the click of the triangular "play" button. That "click of the button," signifying the enactment of our bodies in the world, could have served as the liturgical dismissal.

Mary Lou Baumgartner similarly invited her parishioners to engage their bodies in a new way during a sermon:

> When I was preparing a sermon on Matthew's account of the Feeding of the 5,000 (Mt 14:13–21, Year A Pentecost 18), I sought to highlight the similarities between that story and the account of the Institution of the Lord's Supper by repeating and demonstrating the actions common to both stories (took, gave thanks, broke, gave). I chose the following gestures.
>
> > Took—I stretched out my hands, palms facing upward, and pulled them inward, into fists.
> > Gave thanks—I lifted my hands toward heaven.
> > Broke—I held my hands as though I had picked up a loaf of bread and tore it in two.
> > Gave—I opened my hands, palms facing upward, and stretched them out.
>
> This was the introduction to the sermon. . . .
>
> **Take. Bless. Break. Give.** [I did each of the gestures.] Whenever Jesus feeds his people, these are the four

actions. But the actions are the same. **Take. Bless. Break. Give.** Will you say them with me? **Take. Bless. Break. Give.** Now try it with the actions. I invite you to join me in the actions whenever you hear these words. **Take. Bless. Break. Give.**

After retelling the story with the gestures, I followed the same pattern and used the same gestures to talk about a local summer feeding program for children and a global hunger program of our denomination. Then I repeated the actions as I invited the hearers to take the bread of the Eucharist, blessed and broken for them, and then to go out to give the bread of life to others.[22]

Australian pastor Linda Hamill offers an example of evoking embodied participation that is less overt. She acknowledges her people's struggles "during the time in which much of Australia was burning" by "pointing out my own struggles":

> For me Christmas was a bunch of mixed feelings. The kids came, it was fun, but my friends and colleagues were dealing with tremendous disasters in their communities.

In response to these mixed feelings, near the end of the sermon after the hope of the text of John 1 had been described, I offered time for meditation during the sermon,

> I invite you to sit now, be held by God close to God's heart, in God bosom. Feel the warmth, the comfort the love. Sit in hope, sit in light and see God's glory shine round.

I then allowed a minute of silence before concluding the sermon. Many people thanked me for the opportunity to slow down, to stop and experience God. By stopping and taking the pulse of people in the congregation by asking what they wish they would hear in a sermon, my preaching becomes far more relevant addressing the issues where hope is required.[23]

Instead of encouraging her congregation members to go home and meditate, one of the moves in her sermon was to invite them to meditate then and there . . . together. Once practiced, the body remembers the experience of the meditative stance so that its benefits might be practiced beyond the liturgy.

The difficulty for us to acknowledge the body is due in part to the profound influence on Western thought of a body/spirit dichotomy. René Descartes, for one, prioritized the immaterial (spirit) over the material (body). We in the church forgot to use our bodies even though we speak of our collective being as a body, the body of Christ. But the body of Christ matters. Bodies matter. The particularities of our bodies matter in preaching as well.

Whose Bodies Are Seen and Heard Matters

The examples above offer ways of engaging individual bodies and the body of Christ as a whole during the sermon. Here we broaden the conversation to consider the question of whose bodies are seen and heard during the sermon and why that matters. As more people are invited to speak and act during the sermon, so too will there be broader representation of whose bodies are seen and heard. This broader representation honors diversity, encourages mutual influence, and creates a sense of belonging.

Representation is perhaps less about what we do with our bodies and more about the particularities of the bodies that are participating. Whose bodies are front and center in your worship settings? Whose bodies are seen and heard? Whose bodies seem to take the lead during preaching? Have you considered that a person's identity preaches? Perhaps you've heard the story of the young boy—we'll call him Jake—who had grown up in a congregation with a female pastor. When it was announced that their new pastor would be Scott, the young boy was aghast: "Mommy, a man can't be a pastor, can he?" Or take, for example, the difference in impact between a preacher who proclaims the full acceptance of LGBTQ+ people in the church and an LGBTQ+ person proclaiming Jesus's acceptance of us. A person's identity can have just as much impact as the words of the sermon. In Aristotelian terms, "identity" is related to *ethos* and the "word" to *logos*. Aristotle, and numerous preachers since, have argued that both *ethos* and *logos*, along with *pathos*, impact audiences.

While not every congregation has the luxury of a diverse pastoral staff, most congregations reflect some kind of diversity, whether in gender identity, age, race, sexual orientation, primary language, or other characteristics. Seeing the bodies and hearing the voices of this diverse representation connected to one of the church's quintessential practices—preaching—honors the diversity of God's beloved in more profound ways than simply saying, "The diversity of God's beloved is honored here." The complexity and diversity of human identity at work is the *imago Dei* at work.

We've recognized people's different "ways of knowing" and have therefore sought ways to avoid "the oppressive use of language that assumes there is only one way to see and respond to the vast and many-angled complexity of human life."[24] We've accepted that because "the preacher's experiences and articulations are never universal and normative, they need the corrective of the multiple experiences of God's people."[25] And yet to "situate preaching as radical act of compassionate responsibility,"[26] we must move beyond seeking a corrective simply through awareness to actually expanding those who are seen in the pulpit and whose voices are heard from the pulpit.[27]

Those bodies that are involved in the preaching ministry of a congregation have influence, both within the faith community and beyond. Imagine the possibilities when a pastor is open to the influence of a parishioner. One pastor shared (with permission) the reflections of a parishioner who speaks about preachers who are willing to hear feedback on their preaching. Gloria Foster from Grace Lutheran Church in Wanatchee, Washington, says, "[Preachers] being vulnerable to critique from participants on the sermon presented the previous Sunday makes the entire group unafraid of sharing their thoughts and feelings." The role of sermon feedback will be the focus of the next chapter, but note how this parishioner speaks about the impact of having influence on her pastor's preaching and perhaps sometimes even the sermon itself. When human identities of all varieties have influence, humanity is uplifted and honored.

Mutual influence and authority work together. Recall from chapter 2 that we asked, By what authority does someone preach? Here we also ask, Who has the authority to be in front of the assembly? Who has the authority to speak? What authority do some people have that others do not? Why? To what extent is shared authority a Christian commitment? Is there room for a shared authority for the sake of mutual influence? To what extent is the conversation around authority and influence applicable to a community's preaching ministry?[28]

Whichever phrase is used—"broaden participation," "pass the mic," or Schüssler Fiorenza's "relinquish [the] monopoly"—to describe a new way forward is less important than seeing it in action. For when we honor people's particular identities and encourage their capacity to influence, they will likely experience a sense of belonging, which is a basic human need (see chapter 3 above). Since one of the church's calls is arguably to care for basic human needs, we can add "offer a sense of belonging" to the essential list: feed the hungry, heal the sick, clothe the naked, visit the imprisoned. Where the structures of our practices implicitly (perhaps sometimes explicitly) contradict these aims, we have room to grow. Our preaching practices have room to grow.

Lay Preachers

One of the ways the church has room to grow is to expand its cadre of preachers to include wholeheartedly lay preachers. If preachers trust their congregation members to proclaim out in the world, why not in the sanctuary? I often get the question from nervous preachers, "So you mean I have to 'give up the pulpit'?" I hope the examples above of broadening participation during the sermon assuage such concerns. While, yes, I am challenging a singular "ownership" of the pulpit, preachers still have the responsibility of "stewarding" the pulpit. To be clear, this not an opportunity for the pastor to abandon preaching responsibilities altogether, especially since they made promises to preach at their ordination.

My proposal is somewhere between the thinking of Lucy Atkinson Rose, who says she does not mean to suggest worshippers will preach during the set-aside time in the liturgy, and Elisabeth Schüssler Fiorenza, who called for the clergy to "relinquish their monopoly of the pulpit."[29] Does "passing the mic" have to mean that laypeople preach more often? Not necessarily. Could it? Yes. The question becomes, what will nourish people in their walk of discipleship? Most people will not become part of the preaching rotation. Again, not everyone is called to preach in a worship setting. But the next person might be. What an amazing testimony to the power of the gospel it is when congregation members have been solidly equipped to preach when the pastor is on vacation.[30]

When called preachers "pass the mic" in a congregation, they become teachers of preaching. As such, they mentor and equip others to competently and confidently proclaim the gospel both in their lives and perhaps even from the congregation's pulpit. So, you see, the one who promised to bear responsibility for faithful proclamation in a community still has a role.

Anyone who becomes involved in a community's preaching ministry takes on the responsibility and expends the effort to understand what preaching is, why the church preaches, and how to preach faithfully. The called preacher can guide people through this learning process. My hope is that encouraging these efforts will calm anxieties around the biggest charge against the preaching of laity—that is, the potential for disseminating "bad theology."[31] Again, I am not arguing for "open mic" time during which people say what they will.[32] Rather, called preachers must steward the pulpit by equipping others to preach, and to do so faithfully. Of course, lay preachers also bear responsibility to broaden their conversation in ways that this book proposes. Former (!) Lone-Ranger preachers who have abandoned habits of "going it alone" will want to encourage their lay preachers to "pass the mic" right from the start.

Objectors to a lay preaching movement might note that lay preaching is already a reality in many churches around the world. Even in the United States, robust lay preaching occurs in the chapels of our denominational colleges and universities. The task now before us is to equip these preachers to proclaim faithfully and confidently.

Testimonials from the Congregation

Because it would be disingenuous of me not to "pass the mic," I now yield a few pages to a pastor who has taken to heart this call to reform his preaching practice. James Aalgaard, mentioned above, reflects on what it has meant to shed his preconceived notion that preaching was entirely his solo work (a notion admittedly inherited through models and education):

> My own development as a preacher has been a kind of wilderness wandering. Temptations and stretches of solitary time made the task of proclamation a difficult one. The gift that helped me out of the wilderness was community gathered actively and dynamically around the Word.
>
> My temptation, like a lyricist, to choose just the right word or turn of phrase made for long hours sitting in front of my computer—usually most of Saturday. I knew intuitively that the intent of that grindingly slow work was to have something life-giving and fresh to say, but truth be told, by the time of my in-person delivery, I was just plain exhausted. I realized I had been writing

something for a reading audience, not so much preparing a sermon for hearers within living worship. I didn't know how to find my way out.

Long stretches of solitary time was another problem for me. . . . I was to be somewhat set apart yet at the same time, I was supposed to know and connect deeply with people. I was lonely, and I had indoctrinated myself with the idea that sermon preparation was my work, and mine alone. Isn't this what it means to earn a living?

Before learning about and putting some of these tools of engagement into practice . . . , a strange thing would tend to happen in my weekly ministry. When I got out of my office and into people's homes, when I nurtured community relationships, when I interacted with others as pastor, sibling in Christ and community member, for some odd reason it was easier to prepare my sermon. I didn't even have to mention any of the texts [when I talked with people]! Something about these interactions loosened up my spirit, got me out of my own head and nudged me out of the wilderness.

Inviting the community into the proclamation has been a game-changer. We have consistently held a weekly lectionary study where we begin by thinking back to the Sunday prior, asking how the sermon or other part of the worship has perhaps "grown legs." I frequently remind participants that sermons are never really finished. After review, we read from the texts to come, sometimes dwelling on the Prayer of the Day, sometimes slowly "chewing on" hymn texts. The responses, insights, and wonderings of the participants are always so valuable. As an internship supervisor, one of my goals is to help each intern experience this type of study and engagement, so they can begin their ministry with a spirit of collaboration, truly living out what it means that the proclamation of the gospel is the work of the people.

My favorite tool for engagement is either the literary practice, or its neighbor, the empathetic. It takes guts for participants to write a few thoughts in meditative silence from the perspective of a character from the story. . . . Next, people are invited to share their reflection if they would like. To hear a ninety-year-old widow reflect on what it would be like to be Mary visited by an angel . . . this brings tears to my eyes and provides a depth that I could never fully appreciate. To hear a retired music teacher reflect on what it must be like to be a child raised to new life, well, that's enough sermon in itself. To listen as a relatively shy, introverted middle-aged mom wonders aloud if she would be able to speak prophetically like John the Baptist—and then write a moving letter to the editor about the political vitriol happening in our country, this is faith active in love.[33]

In good form, Aalgaard "passes the mic" to his parishioners to offer their reflections on what difference a broadened participation in the congregation's preaching ministry has made for them. Julie Banken, a member of Aalgaard's congregation and an educator in Washington State, writes,

What we do in the lectionary study is very similar to what a good teacher would do in a classroom. In general, our lectionary study follows the same KWL method that I use at school. Before the sermon on Sunday, we share our thoughts and what we know about the readings. Even if we don't know much, we get to spend time asking questions and thinking deeply about the readings, the authors' intent, the historical context, and possible interpretations. The questions I have are what linger for the rest of the week. I always look forward to comparing our Wednesday discussion with the Sunday sermon. The following week, we discuss the sermon and share what resonated with us. Recalling the sermon together brings out new points, as often everyone hears it differently. Best of all, the ideas stick with me.

I have attended the lectionary study for about three years, since it started, actually! Being part of this group has changed how I experience our Sunday worship. The sermon is my favorite part. I listen better, follow along better, and have something to share and discuss with my own family afterward. The sermon somehow lasts all week instead of just fifteen minutes! I know that the sermon is more meaningful thanks to James and the time he has dedicated to the lectionary study. On the weeks that I am not able to attend, I miss it a lot.

Thank you to pastors everywhere who make the lectionary study a part of worship![34]

Participation clearly leads to deeper engagement—even inspiration. Read again the insights of Gloria Foster: "Listening to the following week's sermon and finding thoughts shared from lectionary study completely engages me in the sermon. The best example of how the lectionary study impacts me is [that if I miss it, it's] the same as how I feel if a Sunday goes by without participating in Communion. Just as Communion feeds the soul, so does lectionary study. As the Grace Lutheran Church Mission Statement reads, 'We proclaim and celebrate the gospel of Jesus Christ through word and sacrament so that *a community of believers is created, trained, nurtured and sent into mission.*'[35] These testimonials affirm a practice of preaching that seeks to help people understand their lives by giving them tools rather than doing something for them.[36]

"Virtual" Preaching . . . Really!

When presenting the material in this book in seminary preaching courses and workshops, I encourage students and participants to explore using technology as much as possible—for example, facilitate a Bible study over Zoom, Google Meet, or Skype. "What? A Bible study over Zoom?" Now that we have lived through one full year of the global COVID-19 pandemic, which moved online nearly everything related to church, even worship, we know an online Bible study is possible! (Indeed, the church is not a building but rather a body of people.)

Preachers have figured out ways to engage people online during their sermons: perhaps using the chat, breakout rooms, or the screen-share function. It's quite easy to "pass the mic" when inviting others to be a cohost so that they can share their screens or to be "pinned" in "speaker view." These functions allow easy transitions to another person sharing their insights and stories.

Sermons that are prerecorded "on location" can be quite creative. Tacoma, Washington, pastor Hallie Parkins says that she and her colleagues "have been thinking about context and how the preaching location lends itself to the proclamation (and how location can 'fit' the text in a different way)." Parkins describes some of their creative recording locations:

* For Palm Sunday, we processed through the Tacoma, starting at the bridge/"gate" of the city, pausing at City Hall for the sermon, and ending at the "temple" (a.k.a. the church) for communion.
* For Good Shepherd Sunday, we recorded on a sheep farm—an actual sheep farm. We spent an entire afternoon following/chasing the sheep around the pasture for parts of the sermon. And then I recorded communion kneeling in the pasture (trying to avoid all the sheep poop).

Parkins shared with me an "update on the whole sermon recording/proclamation during a pandemic." She added, "It's gold." These practices need not be "cheesy" or "gimmicky." Think about Jesus going to wells, marketplaces, fields, wharfs. Location. Location. Location. The on-site scenes could still be prerecorded and presented as a move within the sermon. Yes, these clips will have to be cued up differently, but it is possible.[37] Parkins offers additional examples:

* My colleague's sermon during our care-of-creation series on "forest" offers the best example . . . as he weaves in a video clip of a conversation about the interdependence of communities of trees through roots and fungal networks with a parishioner who used to work for Weyerhaeuser, connecting into our relational interdependence (Ezek 17; Ps 104). We're in the middle of a second growth forest, in the middle of forest fire season in Washington. I presided over communion on a nurse log.[38]

✳ My peak moment was climbing up a literal mountain (Mt. Si, a favorite hike of many in the congregation, with a 3K+ ascent) and preaching for Transfiguration Sunday, with clips in the sermon of both me hiking and the sun coming through the trees.[39]

Sermon content can be gleaned by connecting with people in the congregation and engaging the people and environs in the surrounding community. What was once deemed impossible has been fully adapted to virtual preaching. We've discovered that people are adaptable. And they want to participate. The more participatory Web 2.0 world in which we live has shaped our daily interactivity. Some have claimed that "consumer culture" is giving way to a more "participatory culture" or, at least, "prosumption culture," in which people, called prosumers, are both producers and consumers.[40]

I encourage preachers to be in conversation with their congregation about which "best of" practices from online worship they might harness for in-person worship, including the sermon. What a perfect chance to transition from "pinning" other people's videos while they speak on Zoom to inviting them to the pulpit to share in the proclamation. The ability to show up once again to worship with our whole bodies as the body of Christ is an opportunity not to be missed. My hope is that we will harness this unprecedented transition from being squares on a screen to whole bodies together in holy places in ways that will incarnate—that is, put flesh on—God's word.

For Reflection and Discussion

1. Identify the ways various people in your worship setting are invited to participate *during* the sermon.
2. Which of the possibilities named above might work in your setting and why?
3. Whose bodies are seen and heard most often in your congregation's preaching ministry?
4. To what extent might it be possible to broaden representation? Or, what keeps you from broadening representation?

6

Feedback
Beyond Ego Strokes and Ego Strikes

"Now what?" is the motivating question for this chapter. What happens now that you've engaged in communal Bible study and preached a sermon that incorporates discoveries from that feedforward process and perhaps even "shared the mic" with others? Many preachers might answer, "Now it's up to the Holy Spirit." Indeed, the Holy Spirit will work through the community members as they are sent out into the world. I also think the Holy Spirit can and will work in and through an intentional feedback process. This situation is not a case of either/or; it is not that either we work or the Holy Spirit works. Just as we pray the Holy Spirit would be active through the communal feedforward process, we pray the Holy Spirit would infuse a communal feedback process.

As compelling as it is to put the sermon behind us right after we preach it, not joining the Holy Spirit in the important follow-up work seems to be a missed opportunity on numerous levels. First, when preachers follow up with their listeners after a sermon is preached, they begin to understand if what they hoped people would hear was actually heard. Second, when preachers facilitate occasions for listeners to offer postsermon feedback, the congregation begins to develop the confidence and competence to continue the conversation. After all, don't preachers hope that what they say will not remain in the sanctuary but will be carried out into the world by others?[1] The goal of this chapter is to equip preachers and congregation members alike to continue the conversation after the sermon has been preached.

Most people who took a preaching class in seminary participated in a feedback process in which classmates filled out feedback forms during and after listening to one another preach and then "circled up" to flesh out this feedback in conversation. The written portion of the process has lived on in some contexts with required confirmation "sermon notes." But why get feedback only from confirmation students? Without excluding these young adults, why not ask for feedback from people of all generations? And why not invite such feedback regularly?

The proposed feedback process is not about giving the preacher ego strokes or ego strikes. To be sure, there are times when ego strikes are necessary; preachers need correctives too. And, of course, ego strokes are nice; preachers need affirmation too. This process is not only about the preachers, however. It is also about the listeners, the preacher's partners, in order to equip them to do much more than "listen." Some preachers are disappointed that they do not receive deeper, more meaningful feedback beyond "Nice sermon, pastor!" or "Thank you for enunciating. I could hear every word!"[2] But I wonder how, or even *if*, preachers have equipped congregation members to offer the deeper feedback they desire, feedback that is actually feedforward fodder for Christian discipleship in the world. Discipleship in the world is just one of a number of reasons facilitating occasions for postsermon conversation is important.

Why

Utilizing sermon feedback forms and hosting postsermon conversations are prudent and faithful ministry practices for a variety of reasons, including to "get the gospel heard," to repair communication breakdowns, to empower and equip the laity, and to develop mutual ministry.

Getting the Gospel Heard

It is commonly said that the preacher's task is not only to preach the gospel but to get the gospel heard.[3] How are preachers to know if the gospel is heard if they don't ask the listeners? Preachers often assume listeners hear good news. And they must think everything they say is relevant to people's lives—otherwise they would not say it. And yet some listeners are quick to say they did not hear good news or, worse, the sermon content is not relevant to their lives. Note the word *assume* above. Unfortunately, communication breakdowns are inevitable. But having a feedback process in place increases the chance to repair them. The stakes are high, since the good news of Jesus is that important!

The Christian tradition to which I belong, Lutheranism, assigns great importance to the distinction between God's word as law and God's word as gospel. This law/gospel dialectic is particularly important for preachers. Unfortunately, however, it is often misunderstood to be about what the preacher intends when it is actually about the impact God's word has on the listener—that is, what experience they have when hearing the words. This notion is tricky. The same word(s) uttered in a sermon might be experienced by one person as law and by another as gospel. Same word. Same occasion. Different people. It could also be the case that a person experiences a word as law on one occasion and gospel on another occasion. Same word. Same person. Different occasion. How will we know if God's word and our proclamations of God's word are received as liberating (gospel) or condemning (law) if we don't ask? I might hope for people to hear loudly and clearly that God has graciously claimed them as their own and will not leave them, but someone indicates on a feedback form, "I fall short of God's will for my life and will work harder to do better so that God will love me." In that case, as the preacher, I have some follow-up work to do in order to communicate the good news of God's grace more effectively. I can most certainly do so in future sermons. I might also consider inviting more conversation with the individual.

Unfortunately, we preachers make too many assumptions, and communication breakdowns often lead to misunderstanding, unhelpful theologies, and perhaps even dwindling commitment. Each of these results might impede an individual's life of discipleship as well as the church's mission in the world. Encouraging feedback in a variety of forms helps preachers become aware of how and what their listeners hear so that the intention and impact of a sermon align.

Repairing Communication Breakdowns

We cannot possibly know all of the communication breakdowns that happen between pulpit and pew, but that does not mean we should not try. The sermon feedback process offers opportunities both to learn about these breakdowns and, very importantly, to repair them. Because of the inherent authority that the office of the preacher carries (whether or not it seems that authority has dwindled and whether or not preachers want that authority, it is still there), the preacher should initiate a process for feedback.

I suspect most of us with inherent authority in situations have been tested when others misunderstand the points that we have so delicately and diligently designed so that they would make sense to others. We get trapped in what Reuel Howe referred to as "monological illusion," the notion that communication happens when people "tell others what they ought to know."[4] This misconception about the nature of communication misses one of the basic principles of dialogue between two people—openness to the other. Both parties have a right to speak and have the responsibility to listen. We both have something to offer. We all have much to learn. Perhaps teaching has an advantage over preaching during worship because of its back-and-forth dialogue nature in the classroom setting. Teachers can attempt to repair communication breakdowns in the moment.

I want to share an example of a communication breakdown in which I wrongly assumed that a phrase had the same meaning and impact for all people. Frankly, I didn't even really think about it ahead of time (which means I assumed), and that was my mistake. I was telling students about a time when I was a parish pastor and preaching. In the middle of the sermon, there was some commotion in the pews, which led to some agitated physical movement and some raised voices (not typical in that setting). Mrs. "Johnson" had fainted, and people were starting to come to her aid as other people shouted for someone to call 9-1-1. I explained to the class that ever since that experience, when I hear raised voices during a sermon, I am immediately triggered and impulsively want to call 9-1-1 for medical assistance. (Even though Mrs. Johnson fainted regularly during sermons, the routine did not make the events any less troubling over time.)

I was sharing this backstory after having been similarly triggered as I listened to an audio recording of a sermon in which
a congregation member was regularly raising her voice. But not
far into my story, some people in the class were not able to hear
what I was saying because for them "call 9-1-1" is not primarily a cry for medical help but rather a demand for the police to
enforce order. Calling 9-1-1, for some, does not restore health, it
impedes one's individual expression and human agency.

Thank goodness someone was empowered to interrupt me
and express concern. Otherwise, I never would have become
aware of the disconnect. Yes, I wanted to say, "But you all know
that's not what I meant. What I meant was . . ." or "You must
know by now that I would never intend that." As both a preacher
and a professor, I've learned (though clearly not perfected) that
one "best practice" for repairing ruptures in communication is
to be compassionately curious. The best response (and by that, I
mean, the response that exhibits more openness to the other)
is to be thankful for the student's boldness and to get curious.
Instead of trying to defend myself, I could respond, "Thank you
for pointing that out. I'm wondering what I said that led you to
hear X." Even better, "Please, tell me more about that." This recommendation is not easy to exercise in the moment, when one
is feeling triggered and perhaps emotionally flooded. Being vulnerable is difficult, especially for those who benefit from more
agency than others. Even so, developing these skills for the sake
of repairing communication breakdowns is itself a spiritual practice worthy of a preacher's attention.

When and how, though, will this repair happen when there
is a communication breakdown between pulpit and pew if there is
no feedback process in place? Had the example above taken
place in a sermon from the pulpit in a congregation that had

no feedback process, I would likely never find out about the communication breakdown and therefore never have a chance to repair it (and, in this case, to admit a need to work on my implicit bias). The result of unrepaired communication breakdowns is a breach of trust, which is a major impediment to getting the gospel heard.

The pulpit is especially susceptible to "monological illusion," as the role of pastor has become more professionalized. "That's what we pay you for" is what preachers anticipate hearing from their congregation members and, indeed, what some have actually heard when they encourage broader participation in a setting's preaching ministry. But are preachers paid primarily to transmit a message like the Greek god Hermes, whose access to the divine beings and the mortals meant he was the go-between, the interpreter (thus our word *hermeneutics*)? Might the person in the pulpit and the people in the pew alike have access to the divine? Might they stand together in awe over God's word just as they might before a majestic work of art and wonder aloud, "What moves you? What resonates with you? What do you think of that? How do you feel when you see that?" Might the preacher's role be to get the conversation started and, only when necessary, gently redirect? Howe's "monological illusion" can move toward dialogical expression.

Linguistic ambiguity, Robert Browne claims, does not keep anyone from speaking their truths; "any truth they speak, however, will always remain ambiguous."[5] Linguistic ambiguity and complexity led Rose to develop a homiletic that recognizes that "all language, including the language of faith, is inevitably biased and limited, historically conditioned, and inseparable from the sins of each generation and each community of users."[6] The conviction that "the language of faith is never innocent or unambiguous"[7]—alongside the belief that "the preacher and the congregation are not separate entities, but a community of faith," who are "equal partners on a journey to understand and live out their faith commitments"[8]—led Rose to claim that "the aim of preaching is to gather the community of faith around the word to set texts and interpretations loose in the midst of the community in order to foster and refocus its central conversations."[9]

Preachers know both the vulnerability and possibility of "setting texts and interpretations loose." They often say, "They told me how much they appreciated the point about 'x,' but I never said that." What a gift is divine intervention when such ambiguity works out positively! But what about those times when something that was heard was not appreciated or not shared? I suspect the disconnect between what preachers intend to say and what listeners hear may have been an impetus for a major study on preaching begun in 2001 by Christian Theological Seminary in partnership with the Lilly Foundation, which was the first large-scale qualitative study of people who listen to sermons:[10] "According to this survey, pastors generally think that they are addressing people's real-life circumstances, whereas many listeners see the preacher as a 'like a hovercraft,' floating over particular issues but not interacting with them directly."[11] Lori Carrell's study, too, found that "preachers and listeners have different goals for what happens during the sermon time" and that "preachers have misconceptions about what listeners want from a sermon."[12] Getting on the same page about expectations (or at least knowing what page the other is on) from the start can be helpful. Even so, there will be gaps between what is said and what is heard.

The inevitability of communication breakdowns calls for occasions to give preaching partners a chance to offer their "counterproposals" to the preachers' "proposal," to use the language of Lucy Atkinson Rose.[13] Church historian Mary Jane Haemig expresses the important role of the laity in this way: "Consideration of who God is and what God does is not left to the theologians."[14] More than getting the gospel heard, the task becomes figuring out *together* what the gospel is! People will be empowered and equipped to fulfill this task when preachers elicit postsermon feedback and conversation.

Empowering and Equipping the Laity

Regarding the church's preaching ministry, the laity has been disempowered. Perhaps they've never known they've had homiletical agency. Or perhaps they've known but did not know how to participate. Or, worse, perhaps they have felt their thoughts would not be well received. Most ministry contexts will need leaders to work on both empowering and equipping. Feel free to dream about the alternative to a disempowered and ill-equipped laity. I have. I dream about preaching partners having a chance to practice using theological language and articulating the gospel in safe and bold spaces. I imagine preachers getting immediate feedback from others, through both verbal expression and nonverbal cues, on how their perspectives land. I imagine a preacher's delight when they learn from others what "works" in sermons for them. I dream about the day when the laity are empowered to speak in front of and listen to one another about the sermon they just heard. My dream is that the *homileo*-ing that began in the feedforward groups and continued in the pulpit will be sustained in the lives of preaching partners as they broadcast God's living word in the world.

Take a moment here to consider and converse about the following questions:

What is the history of the role of the laity in your own tra-
dition? More particularly, what is the history of the role of
laity around preaching in your tradition? In your worship-
ping community?

The work of empowering the laity, while often forgotten
(or assumed!), is not new. My own tradition has occasionally
forgotten that Martin Luther, who argued that all Christians
were priests, challenged ecclesiastical hierarchy with the question "Why should we not also have the power to test and judge
what is right or wrong in matters of faith?" According to Haemig, Luther concluded that "it is the duty of every Christian to
espouse the cause of the faith, to understand and defend it, and
to denounce every error. . . . He asserted that 'all Christians are
priests in equal degree,' and included among the functions of
a priest to 'judge of all doctrines and spirits.'"[15] Her research on
the empowerment of the laity during the Protestant reformation
led her to assert, "The reformers did not think that the great
battles of faith were fought only by the clergy, the hierarchy, or
prominent saints in the past."[16]

Still, it is one thing to declare that people are empowered and yet another thing altogether to empower them with
skills. Many preachers have said in a sermon at one point or
another something to the effect of "Now you, children of God,
go out and proclaim the good news." And then they wonder
why the listeners don't actually do it. Rather than point fingers at "them," I've started to realize that it is we preachers who
have failed to equip our congregation members to do so. During the reformation, "ordinary Christians needed weapons for
use in the ongoing fight against all that could destroy faith and
cause the Christian to despair."[17] Those "weapons" (though I

prefer less militaristic language for the work of empowering and equipping) included (1) Scripture translated into the vernacular and (2) the catechism.

In order for the priesthood of all believers to fulfill its duties, all needed access to Scripture. So Luther translated both the Hebrew Scriptures and New Testament into the language of the people. In part, this access to Scripture assisted all Christians to fulfill the "functions of a priest to 'judge of all doctrines and spirits.'" Indeed, in order to "defend" the "cause of faith," one must have the capacity to do so. Therefore, an educated laity—more specifically, educated with regard to Scripture—was central to Luther's reforms. "Back to the sources," *Ad fontes*, was a Reformation rallying cry. So, too, today. We would do well to get back to the basics regarding how to read Scripture in order for people to gain the competence and confidence they need to participate in postsermon conversation and proclamation in the world.[18]

Where illiteracy predominated in the sixteenth century, the catechism aimed to fill in the gap.[19] While catechisms were *de rigueur* in the sixteenth century, Luther set out to write his own. It is not insignificant that Luther penned the Small Catechism first. The Small Catechism was to be used in homes and schools as well as congregations; in other words, it was written for laypeople to teach other laypeople. Luther also emphasized the education of women and young girls, which was not inconsequential for his time.[20]

Luther exhorted all to fulfill their role to learn as well as *teach* the catechetical material. For example, in one of his 1,528 sermons on the Ten Commandments, Luther insisted, "Every father of a family is a bishop in his house and the wife a bishopress. Therefore, remember that you in your homes are to help us carry on the ministry as we do in the church."[21] Everyone is a student as well as a teacher of the faith. Luther taught, says Haemig, "Oversight of preaching and teaching resided with all Christians, not just a clerical subgroup."[22] Even "ordinary people, if given tools, can understand Scripture," thereby making them "independent of the whims and caprices of pastors, priests, and false teachers."[23] The endeavor is about empowerment and not indoctrination. Haemig continues, "Knowing the catechism empowered laypeople to evaluate what they heard—and provided the laity with an important ecclesiastical oversight function. The catechism empowered laity to listen intelligently to sermons and also empowered them to distinguish between true and false teaching, that is, to judge what was being preached and taught to them. This view was revolutionary in its time, both socially and ecclesiastically! The Reformers wanted intelligent, engaged listeners, not passive acquiescence."[24]

Specifically related to our purposes here, Haemig claims that "one purpose of teaching the catechism was to produce thoughtful hearers of sermons." She tells of one Simon Musaeus, who urged his congregation to study the catechism, since it "shows them the right way to understand their sermons" and "gives to listeners a certain 'touchstone and scale to distinguish the damnable lies and many corruptions from the salvific truth.'"[25]

Above all, "The Lutheran enterprise of catechizing—whether done by preaching or teaching—assumed the role of pastor is to empower the laity to know the faith and discern its consequences in their lives."[26] Haemig challenges present-day systems in which laypeople do not have a voice. I, too, encourage challenging these systems by equipping people to read Scripture and think and speak theologically (through catechisms, for example, as well as other kinds of Christian education), so that they might desire and be empowered to participate in postsermon feedback and conversation as a model (and practice) for doing so as disciples in the world. A hoped-for result will be the development of an empowered and empowering mutual ministry.

Developing Mutual Ministry

Lucy Atkinson Rose asserts that one obstacle to preaching's goal of "gathering the community of faith around the Word" is the "gap" between pulpit and pew. Therefore, Rose seeks preaching that is "rooted in a relationship of connectedness and mutuality between preacher and the worshippers."[27] She turns to the work of theologian Rebecca Chopp, who notes that interpretation takes place within a "dialogical community" that "reasons together in order to deliberate its ongoing practices." It is in this kind of community, one that engages in "ongoing discourse and dialogue," that "the freedom to speak is nourished and strengthened."[28]

The "task" of being pastor "involves mutual edification and support," according to Rudolf Bohren.[29] "Solidarity" within the community becomes, in turn, "a paradigm for solidarity with the world: and with creation."[30] Based on Rose's engagement with Bohren's understanding of ministry is her insistence that preaching "upbuilds the congregation as an ongoing, interactive community."[31]

Mutuality and solidarity between preachers and congregation members require trust. For what is still "one of the most extensive investigations into listener preferences in preaching," Hans Van Der Geest interviewed more than two hundred people in Switzerland about "factors in preaching that help them feel engaged in the sermon." Van Der Geest found that "the basic ingredient for successful communication is a sense of trust between preacher and people."[32] Allen, too, in his study

"Listening to Listeners," found that "about 40% of the interviewees listen to the sermon through ethos." Ethos is "the perception that the preacher is a trustworthy person and source," as well as "a sense of relationship with the preacher."[33]

We turn now to considering how greater trust and a sense of relationship between preachers and congregation members (as well as the other benefits noted above) can be strengthened through eliciting sermon feedback and encouraging postsermon conversations.

How

Most often preachers receive feedback informally—through body language during the sermon and after worship, via the brief exchange of words in the "receiving line," or perhaps over coffee at the "fellowship hour" following worship. Sometimes feedback is solicited more intentionally—for example, by placing a "suggestion box" where people can place anonymous notes or identifying a few lay leaders to "have an ear to the ground."

The proposal here is for a transparent, nonanonymous process that deliberately invites a diverse group of people to develop their capacity to reflect on the sermon and share their insights with the preacher and one another, essentially to continue the conversation beyond Sunday morning. Communities that engage in such a feedback process "model ways of legitimizing a variety of personal experiences, interpretations, and convictions as primary ingredients in the community's ongoing conversations."[34] I recommend inviting people to offer feedback both in writing and orally. The written mode will be through feedback forms that people fill out either during or after the sermon. The oral mode of receiving feedback sets up in-person (or virtual, if necessary) group conversations, a form of John McClure's "sermon roundtables," in order to facilitate communal interactions. Both modes require logistical and content-oriented preparation.

Written Feedback: Feedback Forms

When developing a process for written feedback, keep in mind these logistical considerations.

LOGISTICS

1. Who has access to the forms?
2. How and when will they have access?
3. How will they identify themselves?
4. How and when will they return the forms?
5. Will the preacher follow up? If so, how? When?

One "best practice" is to make the feedback form available to all, as well as to get a concrete commitment to complete them from a handful of people. Asking for a commitment allows the preacher to request feedback from people with a variety of backgrounds. The latter is important to reach a cross section of the community, including one's fiercest backers and consistent naysayers. Asking individuals for a commitment to fill out the form also gives the preacher the opportunity to affirm the voices of those who otherwise are not heard. The direct "ask" is a bid for connection and an affirmation that goes a long way in ministry as it communicates, "You matter." Imagine if your preacher had said, "Hi, _____, I'd love to know what you think. Would you be willing to be one of my preaching partners in a couple of weeks?"

Since finding this group of committed responders each week can be taxing, preachers might consider asking for an extended commitment of three or four weeks or, perhaps, for a liturgical season (e.g., Epiphany or the Easter season). It is always good to acknowledge that it's OK if someone has to miss a Sunday or two. Remember, this is an invitation, not a burden. At some point, a few laypeople could assist the preacher in following up with these groups, perhaps checking to see if there are any questions or concerns. The mutuality need not be between only preacher and congregation members but can be among congregation members as well.

In order for all to access feedback forms, consider distributing them electronically ahead of time. Email or post them on the church's website or social media. Early and electronic distribution assists both those who prefer to have the questions in mind ahead of time and those who might prefer to type their responses after worship. I also recommend having a stack of printed feedback forms available on Sunday morning. They could be available for people to pick up as they enter the sanctuary, placed in the pews, or inserted in the bulletin. Think twice before having ushers hand them out along with the bulletin. Sometimes worship attendees will feel self-conscious about saying, "No thank you." Again, being invitational and not overbearing is key.

An oral invitation and an expression of gratitude at the beginning of worship go a long way toward building the rapport needed for this "new thing" to be effective. Preachers will want to assure people that participating in the preaching ministry is completely optional. We don't want to mislead people into thinking this is how they can air their gripes; we want to convey that it is about equipping them for Christian discipleship by playing a vital role in continuing the conversation. Take some time to consider the oral invitation that will be most useful for a particular context. Perhaps the following example will spark some thoughts: "As always, you are invited to participate in our sermon feedback process. There is more information in the bulletin, but I want to highlight that here at [First Presbyterian], we believe the ministry of proclamation belongs to all of us, and this process is one way to affirm that. You are invited to fill out feedback forms and to participate in our roundtable discussion later today in person or on Monday night via Zoom. The community's participation in this ministry benefits us all, so thank you." If oral announcements are not a part of the liturgical culture, simply have the statement printed in the bulletin or displayed on the screen.

Both printed paper and digital options can be effective. While electronic survey templates like those offered by Survey Monkey have become popular, I think it's most beneficial for people to fill out the forms as the sermon is happening (or just after). In fact, this kind of feedback can be understood as an act of worship as we offer our thinking, feeling, and acting selves to the process.

Some (perhaps most) people will prefer just to listen and think about the questions later. That is perfectly fine; don't push them otherwise. Again, be invitational—not overbearing; let people do what works best for them. In fact, comparing and contrasting the feedback received immediately after worship (which presumably was filled out during or immediately after the sermon) and the feedback received up to a week later can be illustrative. Preachers might notice that listeners' capacity to identify theological concepts wanes the further one gets from the preaching event. On the flip side, preachers might notice that listeners' capacity to lean into their world (e.g., by praying for others and identifying their own change/development) increases the farther they get from the sanctuary, when they are more fully reengaged in the world.

CONTENT

Considerations regarding content on the feedback form include the following:

1. Types of questions/prompts
2. Format of questions/prompts: for instance, open-ended questions, rating scales (1–5)
3. Layout of questions/prompts
4. Where to provide one's name and contact info

Regarding the last prompt, identifying oneself on the form is crucial, since this feedback is different from an anonymous note dropped into a suggestion box. Consider it part of the pastoral work to get to know members of the community by continuing the conversation about the sermon with them, which, in turn, encourages their life of discipleship. Anonymity does not work for any of these ministry practices.

One option would be to include a place on the form where the respondent can indicate a desire for follow-up. For example,

Check if applicable:

☐ I would appreciate a follow-up conversation with the preacher.

☐ I would welcome a chance to participate in a regular sermon conversation group.

If checked, please provide your preferred phone number or email address: _____

The content of the questions and prompts is critical. As noted above, these forms do not aim to yield ego strikes or ego strokes for the preacher. Even though the responses may provide preachers with valuable feedback on their delivery, we will not ask here about the preacher's eye contact or vocal quality, for example. And, heaven forbid, we're not asking people to rate the sermon by providing an appraisal of "excellent," "good," "could be better," or "I'm never coming back." I realize there could be a place for this kind of evaluative and perhaps even anonymous feedback, but that is not what this chapter (or this book) is about. At this point, the focus is less about the preacher, and more about the listeners and their baptismal call to proclaim and their lives of discipleship.[35] That goal also means avoiding questions such as "How clear was the message?" or "What is the main point of the sermon?"

Instead of asking . . .	Consider asking . . .
Did you like the sermon?	What happened to you as you considered the sermon?
What was the main point of the sermon?	What title would you give this sermon?
Was my theology clear?	According to this sermon, who is Jesus and how is Jesus at work in our world? In what way(s) does this understanding of Jesus resonate with his role in your life?
Was the sermon clear?	What would you like to know more about? How will you go about discovering more?

I hope the difference between the questions in these two columns is clear. Avoid yes/no questions in favor of more open-ended wording. Also, notice that the second column does not ask listeners to evaluate the preacher (or even the sermon). There were no questions like "Did you like it?" "Was I funny?" or "Could you hear me?"[36] Instead, the prompts in the second column honor the listeners' agency to creatively engage the sermon and evaluate their own Christian discipleship.

To be sure, preachers also have much to gain from these forms for their homiletical self-reflection. For example, the completed feedback forms will help preachers (1) assess what needs more emphasis and what needs less attention, (2) recognize what kind of sermon moves resonate most with people (e.g., retelling the biblical story or offering contemporary stories, theological explanations, encouragement through exhortation), and (3) albeit implicitly, develop their delivery. (For example, if listeners seem to miss what preachers think is most important or impactful, perhaps they might want to adjust their eye contact, cadence, vocal expression, or body language at certain points). As important as these things are, however, they are secondary to the emphasis on the listeners, through whom the Holy Spirit is working.

Consider drawing from the following list of questions and prompts:

* Provide a sermon title: "_____"
* What happened to you as you listened to this sermon?
* (Optional addition) Fill in the blank: This sermon _____ me. Please explain your response.
* What did you hear in the sermon that you are eager to share with another person?
* How might your actions change as a result of this sermon?
* For what and/or for whom does the sermon prompt you to pray?
* According to this sermon, who is God / Jesus / the Holy Spirit, and how is God at work in the world? In your life?
* What in the sermon resonates as good news for you?

✳ What in this sermon entices you to learn more about the biblical story?

The first prompt is my favorite, especially since people have indicated how much they appreciate the intrigue it sparks. By not providing a sermon title, I resist assuming what will be most important to and memorable for the listeners and, instead, let them tell me. Those who provide sermon titles often do so with much delight at their own creativity. I delight with them (and, at the same time, glean some valuable information).

Notice how the questions are open-ended and not simply "yes/no" questions. Also, they are not about evaluating the preacher but continuing the conversation that the sermon has begun. Additionally, notice how they invite people to consider how their whole person is affected. Think again of the Shema in Deuteronomy—we are to love the Lord our God with our "whole beings" (*nefesh* in Hebrew). The question "What happened to you . . . ?" is not typical, since people aren't used to thinking about how a sermon will do something to them beyond making them think (or perhaps, proverbially, "comforting the afflicted" or "afflicting the comfortable"). But God's word has the capacity to do so much more. This question is uniquely linked to a preacher's function statement, since both identify what might happen to a person in the preaching moment.[37]

Next, notice that some questions seek to equip people for theological reflection about the identity of God, the Bible, discipleship, proclamation of the gospel, the beloved community, and ethics. Asking, "For what and/or for whom does the sermon prompt you to pray?" is a way to encourage people to connect their experience of worship with their world. The same is true about the following questions: What did you hear that you are eager to share with another person? And how might your actions change as a result of this sermon?

Finally, the variety of questions aims to connect to the three categories often used to analyze communication events: logos, ethos, and pathos. In their "Listening to Listeners" study, Allen and his team noted, "About 40% of the interviewees in the study group listen to the sermon primarily through its content. For them, the actual theological content of the sermon is paramount. About 40% of the interviewees listen to the sermon through ethos. However, for these people ethos is more than the perception that the preacher is a trustworthy person and source. For them, ethos also includes a sense of relationship with the preacher. About 20% of the interviewees listen to the sermon through pathos. They need to feel the sermon."[38]

See appendix C for sample feedback forms, which you are free to amend as you wish. I encourage you to collaborate with those educators, human resource managers, and communication gurus in your midst who can be your partners in creating the most useful feedback forms for your particular setting.

Oral Feedback: Roundtable Conversations

A group conversation after worship facilitates interaction among preaching partners. Of utmost importance is that this mode of feedback be in real time (either in person or an equivalent online format) and communal (not one-on-one—though follow-up one-on-one conversations after the roundtable can be helpful). This communal, conversational feedback also requires logistical and content-oriented preparations.

LOGISTICS
Logistical concerns include the following:

1. How and when will this conversation be announced?
2. Who will be a part of the conversation?
3. When and where will this conversation happen?
4. Will the seating arrangement be in rows or in a circle?
5. How long will the conversation last?
6. Who will facilitate?
7. Will the preacher follow up? If so, how? When?

Once again, personally inviting people to participate is helpful. First encourage those you personally invited to fill out the feedback form to join the conversation, but do find a way to open up the invitation to anyone who experienced the sermon. Even if someone never participates, knowing they are invited is a step toward recognizing that they matter, their voice is important, and they belong.

This roundtable conversation can be effective with only three and as many as fifty people. The seating arrangement is definitely a concern as the number of participants increases. If possible, meet in a room that is big enough to set the chairs in one big circle so that people can see one another. Remember, a roundtable is not about one person being either in the "hot seat" or "the leader" in the front of the room; it is about the practice of communication, of mutual conversation. If time permits, breaking out into small groups is a good idea as long as one person in each group is willing to take notes and report back to the group. Meeting soon after Sunday worship for seventy-five to ninety minutes is ideal.[39]

The COVID-19 pandemic in 2020 motivated communities to meet via online platforms and, lo and behold, people were able to connect with one another on screen. Therefore, I would not discount the value of holding an online feedback conversation as well, especially since breakout groups are so easy to create online. Be sensitive, though, to the fact that people's energy wanes more quickly in the online format. Therefore, meeting for no more than sixty minutes is ideal for this mode. The online conversation can occur a day or two after worship, which would really give the preacher a sense of what continues to be sustained in the lives of individuals.

A crucial logistical matter is deciding who will serve as the facilitator. It is not uncommon for preachers (and it pains me to have to include myself in this category, but it's true) to want to explain ourselves, or to clarify a point—or, God forbid, to start preaching all over again—if we sense that people "didn't get it." If we tend to grab the mic, then it's best to have someone else facilitate, since these tendencies are surefire ways to communicate to people that we did not really mean we want to hear from them. We preachers had our chance in the pulpit . . . and we'll get another chance the next Sunday. Now it's time to "pass the mic." We may feel vulnerable, yes. But remember, the roundtable conversation is not primarily about us even as it affects us. Being nonanxious and nondefensive helps develop the all-important trust component mentioned above. Think of this part of the process as "letting go of the bicycle" after serving momentarily as the one who assists with balance; delight in the thrill of experiencing your community on this ride with one another as they hear one another speak, learn from one another, and discover models for their own proclamation.

CONTENT

Regarding content, the written feedback form can serve as the foundation for the conversation (whether or not everyone has completed the form). Attending to each question in the order provided can be effective. It is helpful to ask a couple of people who have already completed the form to volunteer their responses first. Then the facilitator can invite others to enter the conversation. Some questions lend themselves to follow-up questions that take the conversation to a deeper level. For example, after letting participants respond to the question "What did you hear that you are eager to share with another person?" the facilitator can simply ask them to say why they answered the way they did. Note that this follow-up prompt aims not to make people feel like they must defend their answers but to elaborate. Also, for the question "How might your actions change as a result of this sermon?" the facilitator can ask, "What in the sermon do you think led you to that response?"

I also recommend adding some questions that did not make it onto the feedback form, such as "What did you want to hear more about?" If small groups are possible, ask yet another question, such as "If you were the preacher, what would you have said?" Ask someone from each small group to report back to the full group one or two highlights from their conversations. Note that this process is about the preaching partners gaining confidence and competence to fulfill their baptismal calls to proclaim. I can't imagine anything more fulfilling to witness as a preacher!

To be sure, things have the potential to go awry. Growth is often not without pains. Just like the sermon is not "open mic" time, this gathering is not "anything goes." I appreciate Haemig's caveat from the Reformation era: "The authority of the layperson to judge all preaching and teaching did not legitimize any judgment that person wanted to make. To the contrary! For the Wittenberg Reformers, this authority was always bound to the Word of God. The catechism was a tool for learning and knowing the Word of God. The Reformers recognized that it is the task of *all* Christians, clergy and lay, to discern what is right and wrong in the faith. All are held accountable to the standards of the apostolic faith, as set forth in Scripture and summarized in creed and confession."[40]

Discerning the word that God is speaking in a particular time and place for a particular people is most effective when *all* Christians, clergy and lay, discern together. But that does not mean people are free to fling judgments at the preacher or one another willy-nilly. Instead, we hold one another accountable even as we are accountable to, as noted in the quote above, "standards of the apostolic faith, as set forth in Scripture and summarized in creed and confession."

I tend to facilitate the roundtable conversation after a student preaches in the preaching classes I teach. I find my taking this role to be very beneficial because it allows the preacher to take in all the feedback without thinking about group dynamics and the time available. But then equally beneficial is allowing the preachers a chance at the end of the session to

* thank the participants for their partnership,
* reflect on what they heard,
* identify what they've learned from others, and
* identify what they will take forward.

Now *that's* mutual ministry, which has a good chance to develop a trusting relationship between preacher and community members. I imagine the conversation itself as the gospel in action. Just as it was for those disciples on the road to Emmaus, whose walking and talking (that is, *homileo*-ing) together was divinely interrupted by Jesus showing up, may it be so for us.

For Reflection and Discussion

1. Describe the sermon feedback process in your ministry setting.
2. What do you think keeps people from "continuing the conversation" that has begun in the sermon?
3. In what ways, perhaps ways described above, would you like to be a part of your congregation's feedback process?

7

Next Steps
Putting It All Together

Worshipping communities that are ready to implement more collaborative preaching practices will experience both immediate and deferred benefits. One of the immediate benefits relates directly to the content of Sunday's sermon. Since feedback from one sermon becomes feedforward for the next sermon, the preacher never begins a sermon with a blank slate. Something might be said in a postsermon roundtable conversation that sparks something for next Sunday's sermon. That something might be related to Scripture (most helpful with continuous lectionary readings), a pastoral concern within the congregation, or, perhaps, a public issue that is on the hearts and minds of many people. Any time sermons arise from the hopes, dreams, thoughts, concerns, confusions, and delights of the congregation, listeners benefit. Another benefit is that as people move from being "listeners" to active "preaching partners," they will increase their biblical literacy, become more confident in telling others about Jesus, and exhibit competence for theological conversation.

One deferred benefit might be the development of a cadre of lay preachers. I suspect that nearly every congregation has one or two people who are not called to go to seminary to prepare for full-time ministry but who have gifts for biblical interpretation and crafting and delivering sermons. What an amazing testament to the power of the gospel it is when congregation members who have been solidly equipped to preach are called upon when the pastor is on vacation or perhaps even more regularly.[1] Is there room for these people (you?) to become a lay preacher in your worshipping community?[2] Understanding and practicing preaching as a ministry of the whole congregation might even result in one or two (or seven) people emerging with a call to full-time ministry.

A good place to start is to identify where you are: "How do you invite your congregation members to participate with you in your sermon preparation process?" When I ask preachers this question, I get responses that vary from "not at all" to "they preach too!" Indeed, listeners and sermons can be connected in many ways. Where does your community fall on this spectrum?

Let the Spirit work.	Listen to member's lives.	Imagine the sermon's impact.	Directly consult listeners.	Lead group Bible studies.	Cultivate preaching partners.	Train lay preachers.

Each of these actions can lead to what we might call "the peoples' sermon." I have no doubt the Holy Spirit has the capacity to do what she will with the proclaimed word. Yet I am encouraging worshipping communities to work toward the right side of the spectrum—that is, to more intentionally collaborate (and to trust that the Holy Spirit will work through that process).

Even if you are with me in theory, you might still wonder about next steps. I offer here some concrete ideas for "putting it all together" by identifying possible next steps for those actions toward the right side of the spectrum and a possible weekly rhythm. Everything proposed here can be adapted to one's ministry context.

One starting point is to begin implementing the actual practices mentioned in previous chapters. For example, in the interest of starting small but hoping for big impact, consider beginning a weekly Bible study based on Sunday's Scripture reading. If such a thing is already offered, then begin to incorporate some of the creative and collaborative exercises from chapter 4 into your study. Another fairly simple addition with big results is to invite a handful of people to fill out a sermon feedback form (see appendix C for samples) and invite them to a roundtable conversation following worship one Sunday.

Other times, however, it helps to begin with theory and then move to practice. By "theory" I mean start with the big picture ideas—the reasons behind the shift. If this direction is more the style of your community, start small by simply having a conversation with a few people about the ideas proposed in this book. You might even consider utilizing a survey, perhaps like Lori Carrell's survey mentioned in chapter 6. Using this or a similar survey will give preachers a sense of how listeners understand preaching. The goal is not for everyone to be on the same page but rather to understand what pages one another are on.

These same people might then become a congregation's preaching partners for a season. For three or four weeks during the Epiphany season, for example, they could join the preacher in the feedforward and feedback process. I recommend that facilitators of these roundtable conversations (likely preachers during the beginning stages) read John McClure's *The Roundtable Pulpit* for a very explicit and helpful guide to working with these small groups. After these few weeks, assess what went well and what could be more effective before involving more people in the congregation.

Another starting point would be to set up a four-week Christian education series on preaching as ministry of the whole congregation. Of course, this book could serve as the foundation for this study. Chapters 1 through 3, in particular, are set up to get that conversation going. You might consider this plan:

Week One: What Is Preaching?
Week Two: Why Preach?
Week Three: Preaching as a Ministry of the Whole
             Congregation
Week Four: Congregational and Biblical Exegesis for
             Preaching

For week one, make your way together through chapter 1 and working definitions of preaching, ending with discussion about expectations, preferences, and commitments about preaching. For week two, make your way together through chapter 2 of this book. Note that if you want to slow things down, this topic could also be explored in three sessions:

1. The biblical basis for preaching
2. The theological basis of preaching
3. Teachings about preaching in the congregation's and its denomination's documents and rites

The first two weeks will lay the foundation for whole-heartedly exploring the notion (and practice!) of preaching as a ministry of the whole congregation, which is the focus of week three. Week three's study could appropriate elements from various chapters in this book in order to reflect on the role of the baptized to proclaim and to equip people to offer their interpretive voices in the sermon preparation process. In other words, instead of the preacher telling people how to understand their lives, the preacher gives them the tools to engage Scripture in order to do so themselves. These tools will give congregation members the confidence and competence to fulfill their baptismal calls to proclaim the gospel.

Chapter 4 will be helpful for the session on week four (Congregational and Biblical Exegesis for Preaching). At this point, preachers can share with their listeners (soon-to-be preaching partners) what their sermon preparation processes have been and then invite them into some of the practices for collaborative biblical exegesis.

I recognize that this outline covers a lot of material for a four-week study. But this tip-of-the-iceberg approach can get the conversation going. Ideally, a small group of people will want to get together to assess the four weeks and explore ways to proceed.

Some congregations will want to allow more time between sessions, perhaps focusing on the church's ministry of preaching for an entire year. I know laypeople are interested in this topic. I also know many hesitate to raise it because "That's the pastor's arena and I don't want to intrude." But a congregational study on preaching for a year would say, "This is *our* arena." Perhaps one could earmark the first Sunday of every month for "Homiletics Class" in the education hour. (Of course, one might need to explain "homiletics." "Preaching Class" works too.) Having a few weeks to read, reflect, and possibly converse before the next class would deepen the study.

If you decide on this theory-to-practice route, my recommendation is that you not wait the full year to begin implementing some of the exercises. The creative and collaborative practices can be integrated into an existing Bible study, offered as a new Bible study, and facilitated in a piecemeal fashion throughout the week. The lowest hanging fruit here is simply to introduce new ways of studying the Bible into an existing Bible study. Pick one new practice at your next Bible study that will take up just fifteen to twenty minutes. For example, introduce the literary exercise (page 92). If you only have five to ten minutes to veer from "the usual," try the "I Wonder / I Notice" exercise (page 86).

If a Bible study based on Sunday's lectionary (or chosen) Scripture readings does not exist, it might be time to begin one. Or perhaps such a Bible study exists but has needed energizing. In either case, a congregation might develop a whole new kind of Bible study, one where the people do the biblical exegesis rather than simply listening to the preacher talk about their exegetical work. Why should preachers get all the benefits of deeply studying God's living word when that word belongs to everyone? Come one and all!

Chapter 4 suggests ways this Bible study can become a regular spiritual practice for participants, just as sermon preparation is a regular spiritual practice for the preacher. The more challenging (though no less fun) part of developing this discipline is choosing which practices to include in a particular Bible study. Careful lesson planning goes a long way. Variety keeps people's interest. Participation yields learning.

Using the KWHL Chart

Lesson planning for the lectionary-based Bible study is where biblical exegesis and focused congregational exegesis come together. In chapter 4, I briefly introduced the KWHL chart, an adaptation of the KWL chart educators use as a process of inquiry that "activates prior knowledge" in order to move toward new discoveries.[3] The KWHL chart exercise (completed as the week goes along) encourages preachers to set aside assumptions in favor of listening to the congregation. Since there is no reason to preach a sermon that is disconnected from the realities of a congregation (as the congregation articulates them), this part of the process is crucial.

What follows is a more detailed account of how one might use the KWHL chart in preaching. You'll see that working with the chart has an added benefit of assisting Bible study leaders in lesson planning—that is, deciding which practices to engage with whom and when.

K	W	H	L
What do I KNOW about the congregation that might shape how they hear Sunday's Scripture readings?	*What do I WANT to know about the congregation that might help me understand how they hear Sunday's Scripture readings?*	*HOW will I find out?*	*What did I LEARN about how the congregation engages this Scripture reading that might have an effect on the sermon?*

The K column invites preachers to consider what they know about the congregation by asking a more pointed question: "What do I *know* about the congregation *that might shape how they hear Sunday's Scripture readings?*" (This might be a good place to stop and fill in the K column on the blank chart provided in

165

appendix B.) Depending on the congregation and Bible story, of course, the column might include the following:

1. This congregation is very committed to social justice.
2. Many people are quick to talk about Jesus's ministry but sometimes question his crucifixion and resurrection.
3. Some members don't appreciate sermons that focus only on the Hebrew Scriptures.
4. Because many people in the community have been to the Holy Land, they love to hear geographical references in the sermon.
5. The congregation is unusually comfortable when the preacher talks about financial stewardship.
6. Like Thomas, many individuals want proof in order to believe in Jesus.

Once you've made that list (add more as necessary as the week goes by), go back and put a check mark by those claims you know for a fact and underline those items that are assumptions. Be honest—you don't have to show anyone your chart. Anything that you underlined automatically gets transferred to the W column, since it becomes something you *want* to know. You might also add more items in the W column as you do your own biblical exegetical work (even if there is nothing in the corresponding K column). Remember, these are things that specifically connect your congregation (the listeners of the sermon) and the biblical story that will serve as the foundation for your upcoming sermon. Here's an example of a start on the column that identifies what you *want* to know.

K	W	H	L
What do I KNOW about the congregation that might shape how they hear Sunday's Scripture readings?	*What do I WANT to know about the congregation that might help me understand how they hear Sunday's Scripture readings?*	*HOW will I find out?*	*What did I LEARN about how the congregation engages this Scripture reading that might have an effect on the sermon?*
They are quick to talk about Jesus's ministry but sometimes question his crucifixion and resurrection.	What do they believe about Jesus's crucifixion and resurrection?		
They resonate with Thomas's doubts and want proof in order to believe in Jesus.	To what extent do they resonate with Thomas's doubts? Do they want proof in order to believe in Jesus?		
	How do they react when others around them question Jesus's resurrection or when others want proof?		

The next step is to ask, "*How* will I find out?" Of course, you could simply call Jane, the most well-connected person in your congregation, and ask her. But we are doing something different here, something more participatory, more communal. We are trying to facilitate exploration of the biblical text, to engage it creatively and collaboratively. We want to gather people around the biblical stories so they can speak for themselves and with one another. Sometimes more indirect and creative practices reveal things that would not have been revealed with a direct question.

I might not even know what I think, but by playing the role of Thomas in the Scripture tableau, for example, I might discover some of my deep-seated beliefs.

Four possible creative and collaborative Bible study practices come to mind that might help me learn what I want to know about the congregation as I prepare the upcoming sermon on John 20. (See the H column in the chart below followed by a possible lesson plan for Bible study.) First, I could lead the "I Wonder / I Notice" exercise with a few different groups during the week—for example, at the beginning of the staff and church council meetings and with the quilting group. Second, in the weekly men's Bible study, I could facilitate the Scripture tableau. With the confirmation students and at the congregational Bible study, I could facilitate the literary exercise (if a confirmation student attends, perhaps he could assist me, since he would have already done the exercise). Fourth, since I think the empathetic exercise will help me with the question "How do they react when others around them question Jesus's resurrection or when others want proof?" I think I'll try it at the congregational Bible study. Speaking of the congregational feedforward Bible study, I offer here a possible ninety-minute lesson plan as a way to suggest a helpful progression of exercises as well as time management.

K	W	H	L
What do I KNOW about the congregation that might shape how they hear Sunday's Scripture readings?	*What do I WANT to know about the congregation that might help me understand how they hear Sunday's Scripture readings?*	*HOW will I find out?*	*What did I LEARN about how the congregation engages this Scripture reading that might have an effect on the sermon?*
They are quick to talk about Jesus's ministry but sometimes question his crucifixion and resurrection.	What do they believe about Jesus's crucifixion and resurrection?	—"I Wonder / I Notice" at the staff meeting (T) and council meeting (Th), with the quilting group (W), and at the congregational Bible study (W). —Scripture tableau with the men's Bible study group (T).	
They resonate with Thomas's doubts and want proof in order to believe in Jesus.	To what extent do they resonate with Thomas's doubts? Do they want proof in order to believe in Jesus?	—Scripture tableau with the men's Bible study group (T) and in congregational Bible study (W). —Literary exercise in congregational Bible study (W) and with confirmation class (W).	
	How do they react when others around them question Jesus's resurrection or when others want proof?	—Literary exercise in congregational Bible study (W) and with confirmation class (W). —Empathetic exercise in congregational Bible study (W).	

00:00–5:00   "I Wonder / I Notice."

5:00–10:00   Debrief the experience.

10:00–35:00   Begin the Scripture tableau (with one or two scenes that could use more work) and then (if permission from the men's Bible study group is granted) share the photographs of their poses for comparison purposes.

35:00–45:00   Debrief the experience.

45:00–70:00   Literary exercise (with some wiggle room in timing for movement).
              5 min.: solo writing
              10 min.: sharing stories in small groups
              10 min.: sharing a few stories in large group and debriefing

70:00–80:00   Prayer: For what or for whom does this study invite us to pray?
              List, then pray.

80:00–85:00   Have each person write on board one exciting discovery and one lingering question.

85:00–90:00   Send people out with an invitation to continue working on their first-person stories and to send them to me if they are willing to share.

Notice that the facilitator never tells the group what the biblical story *means*. This omission is not because the facilitator is withholding but rather because they don't exactly know. The Bible study *is* the process for discovering what the story *means* for these people in this particular time and place.

I have an idea for inviting homebound members to participate even though this activity does not address a specific question in the KWHL chart. I am going to ask those who are willing to let me record them reading aloud the gospel lesson. That way, I'll take their voices with me throughout the week. Since I also want to post something on our congregation's social media platforms, I'll invite the congregation's Facebook followers to read Sunday's gospel reading, find and post a piece of art that best represents their reaction to the story, and write a bit about how the piece represents their experience with the gospel reading.

I would start this process early enough in the week so that it isn't rushed (any more than it already feels). I would commit to working on the sermon a bit each day (about the same amount of time as in my old process, except now I'm collaborating with others). Notice how the feedforward process through the week incorporates the sermon preparation work with regular ministry routines. My week's rhythm of feedforward preaching partners would look like this:

Monday	Tuesday	Wednesday	Thursday	Friday	Saturday	Sunday
—Preliminary exegetical work with the biblical story. (Remember also to complete congregational exegesis worksheet and begin KWHL.)	—"I Wonder / I Notice" at the staff meeting. —Scripture tableau with the men's Bible study group.	—Have homebound members record the reading of the gospel into my phone when I visit them. —Literary exercise with confirmation class. —Weekly congregational Bible study.	—"I Wonder / I Notice" at the council meeting. —Craft a more concrete sermon draft and follow up with any preaching partners whose insights might be a part of the sermon.	—Amend the sermon draft and test any sections I'm unsure about by sharing (orally) with one or two people. (Delivery practice!) —Prepare feedback forms and confirm gathering with feedback roundtable partners.		—Scripture tableau rehearsal if using in worship. —Preach! —Postworship roundtable conversation.

As I make my way through this feedforward process, I write in the chart what I am learning (the L) and incorporate these discoveries as much as possible into the sermon itself. (See appendix B for a sample of a completed KWHL chart.)

I may want to follow up with some of my preaching partners. Perhaps an insight intrigued me and I want to hear more. I may ask some partners if I could use their stories in the sermon. I may even invite them to share their insights during the sermon. Frankly, if nothing finds its way concretely into the sermon itself, what is lost? I've affirmed my sense of where the congregation is in their life of discipleship, or I've been saved from making unfortunate assumptions. I've engaged in Bible study with the congregation. I've found out a bit more about their lives (and have come to know how I might want to follow up pastorally). I've held space for people to speak and listen to one another. By doing these things, I've invited them into the preaching ministry of the congregation. The benefits of "the peoples' sermon" are many. If nothing else, perhaps the process has sparked some people's eagerness for Sunday worship and, in particular, the sermon. I would call that effective. I would call the whole process ministry.

Top Five Tips

My hope is that these final tips will keep you moving forward. But first, I must admit I've not included "pray" as a tip, since praying is less a tip than a way of life. Praying your way into and through this process as your new way of life together is sure to yield deeper relationships with God and with one another. So with that spiritual immersion in effect, I recommend you keep exploring the why, collaborate, communicate, set aside perfectionism, and be patient.

1. Keep Exploring the "Why"

Bearing the responsibility of stewarding the pulpit instead of clutching the privilege of owning it requires a democratization of the whole process in order to hear more voices. Whether we are clergy, lay members, or seekers, we would do well, in Rose's words, to "seek the echoing of contrapuntal proposals of others."[4] Empowering and equipping all people to fulfill their baptismal calls to proclaim God's word is not simply preparation for ministry, it *is* ministry. We embrace our role in the preaching ministry of our worshipping communities as one member of the priesthood of all believers.

2. Collaborate

I cannot promise the yoke will be easy, but any burden of implementing this process will be lighter when the load is shared. Since the whole point is to collaborate with one another, even the development of a new way forward should be collaborative. Pastors, while remaining attentive to your own needs for quiet moments of solitude in order to reflect and regroup, find your preaching partners. Lay members, look for opportunities to become a part of the preaching ministry of your congregation as a preaching partner.

3. Communicate

Because new processes are best begun with advanced notice and plenty of conversation, consider sending a letter to the congregation inviting them to participate. Sample letters to congregations are provided in appendix A. Embrace the recommendations here for sharing current preaching preparation processes, communicating with one another about opportunities for intentional study of preaching as a ministry of the whole congregation, and listening to one another's thoughts and ideas about the new process.

4. Set Aside Perfectionism

Perhaps you have been asked, "What would you do if you knew you could not fail?" But have you ever been asked, "What would you do if you knew you would fail, but it was worth doing anyway?" When I heard author and entrepreneur Seth Godin reframe the question in this way, I thought of preaching as a ministry of the whole congregation. Even if (perhaps I should write *when*) our attempts at a more collaborative preaching ministry fail, what would make the attempt worth it?

The process is just as important, if not more important, than the result. Frankly, I'm quite certain I've never preached a perfect "result." I'm not even sure there is such a thing. The Sunday sermon is less a "result" and more part of the process. An important part, yes, since it is the step in the process that announces, "There is nothing you can do to separate you from God's love." Well, guess what? Not even a preacher's imperfect sermon will separate them from God's love. Not even a preaching partner's less-than-perfect interpretation of a biblical story will separate them from God's love. Not even a circuitous answer on a sermon feedback form will keep someone from God's love. Jesus's death and resurrection have freed us from the self-deprecating sin of judging ourselves so that we might turn toward the neighbor (and ourselves) with a nonjudgmental stance. Jesus's death and resurrection have freed us from having to prove ourselves to others in order to embolden us to pass the mic to them. We have been freed from the need to be perfect so that we might get curious.

"What would you do if you knew you would fail, but it was worth doing anyway?" I'd become a preacher who empowers and equips others to preach. Yes, I might feel vulnerable when I do this new thing because the former (Lone-Ranger) way seemed to work for me. But the new way is worth it.

5. Be Patient

The last thing we want to hear when we are feeling impatient is "Be patient." So I'll say it before you become impatient: "Be patient." Not everything will "take" on the first try when implementing this process. Some things will fail. Establishing a culture of collaboration around a community's preaching ministry takes time. But remember,

> If you want to go fast, go alone.
> If you want to go far, go together.
>
> —African proverb

Let's take our cue from the one who so patiently waits for the beloved, us, to "come and see" then "go and tell" for ourselves. Whether God's decision to invite us to become God's preaching partners is a good idea is not mine to judge. But God does invite us to participate in God's ministry of proclamation even as God declares, "[My word] shall not return to me empty, but it shall accomplish that which I purpose" (Isa 55:11). That assurance empowers the church to let the people preach.

APPENDIX A

Sample Letters to Congregation Members

Dear Friends,

"Will you therefore preach and teach in accordance with the holy Scriptures and these [ecumenical] creeds and confessions?"

As I stood nervously, trying not to cry during my ordination, I answered, "I will, and I ask God to help me." I came to Living Christ Lutheran holding this question close to my heart. The first charge on the Letter of Call you issued me was "Preach God's saving Grace and administer the sacraments." Clearly, this preaching stuff is close to your hearts too!

But I always hold that in tension with a comment a person made to me once: "I don't understand why we have sermons. Couldn't we skip it or have conversation instead?" Truth be told, I have asked similar questions about preaching. There are times when a sermon grabs me and carries me out into the world. Other times, a sermon might carry me back to my bed. Preaching, at its best, both witnesses to God's life and action the world and equips us all to respond in joy to the gospel.

Sometimes the process of sermon preparation is mystifying, even to me. What it is *not* meant to be is the work of just the pastor. It is the work of *all* of us! Yes, even you!

This spring, I will be offering a four-week forum during education time entitled Preaching as a Ministry of the Whole Congregation. Over the four weeks, we will engage questions like "What is preaching?" "Why do we have sermons?" "Does Pastor Kevin need all that time to write a sermon or does he just sit with his feet on his desk all week?" We'll even turn it around and ask "What is my 'skin in the game'?" or "What is my role as the hearer?" You might even think of more as we discern preaching at Living Christ together!

Preaching as a Ministry of the Whole Congregation shapes the way our communal voice is heard on Sundays and within all aspects of the ministry we are called to live into together. Through these interactive sessions, we will explore and discuss how we can find ourselves collaboratively within each message given.

My ordination vows asked if I would preach and teach. When I was installed here, Living Christ declared that we will "strive together in the peace and unity of Christ" in the work of the gospel. I am excited to engage that gospel through the ministry of preaching together and continue to follow the Spirit's call to "do justice, love kindness, and walk humbly with God and neighbor" here at Living Christ.

Be Well,
Pr. Kevin

Dear Shepherd of the Valley Family,

Thanksgiving blessings to you and yours during this time of gratitude! I give God thanks for *you* as a partner and friend in ministry. It has been a wonderful few months getting to know this community, and since day one, I have felt extremely blessed to be called here. As we move into this season of Advent—a time for anticipation, waiting, and yearning—I do hope this new quarterly newsletter finds you and your loved ones feeling the peace of Christ.

Inside you will find a lot of information from us. Some recaps the exciting events that have happened over the last few months, and other information is on how Shepherd of the Valley is looking forward to Advent, Christmas, and 2019! Included as well is the ELCA's Stories of Faith in Action from our partners across the United States and the globe, and a fun Advent activity you can do with your friends, family, or neighbors.

Leading up to Christmas, I will be starting a four-week teaching series in the adult classes on Sundays entitled Preaching as a Ministry of the Whole Congregation. I will also be offering these on Wednesdays throughout, as a multigenerational lesson, as well. I encourage you to attend all four at your preferred time. Time and date details are included on the calendar inside.

After hearing the title of the series, I know what some of you may be thinking: "Am I going to have to get up and preach?!" The short answer is, no (unless you feel called to do so!). Rather, I am hoping together, as a congregation, we can reimagine what it means to preach and reengage with the texts in new and different ways. This will lead us to ask some questions like "Well, what is preaching in the first place?" and "Why do we preach?" Other questions that might arise could be "How does one prepare for a sermon?" or "How long does it take to craft one?" These are fun questions that we will get to answer together.

God calls us to be partners together in ministry. I believe that preaching is the articulation of God and the communication of God's word and certainly something that you have a stake in! By working together, we can share in this Spirit-filled, ancient practice together so that your thoughts, ideas, feelings, and beliefs are uplifted and heard on Sunday mornings too. By working together, collaboratively, we can create a culture where you are able to claim the ministry of preaching as something done not just by me or a few but by everyone in this community . . . *including you!*

This is sacred and holy work and work that I am so excited to engage with you in! Some of you may even feel a strong connection to the lessons on preaching that I will teach and the collaborative process that we learn about, which is fantastic. We'll discuss starting a small group to participate even further—more on that later!

Preaching as a ministry of the whole congregation sounds very difficult and maybe even a little daunting but I promise we will take it step-by-step in an inviting and accessible way for all ages! It is clear that God is working throughout all of us here at Shepherd of the Valley. Let us continue to give thanks and praise to God

for the dynamic ways in which we do divine work with
our hands and voices! Let patience accompany us this
Advent season as we pray, "Christ, we wait for you!"

Peace to you,
Ben Hogue, pastor

APPENDIX B

Sample KWHL Chart

KWHL Chart
Exegeting the congregation in light of Sunday's Scripture: Acts 8:26–39
(Thanks to *Kaari Nieuwlandt*)

K	W	H	L
What do I KNOW about the congregation that might shape how they hear Sunday's Scripture readings?	*What do I WANT to know about the congregation that might help me understand how they hear Sunday's Scripture readings?*	*HOW will I find out?*	*What did I LEARN about how the congregation engages this Scripture reading that might have an effect on the sermon?*
1 The congregation is a Reconciling in Christ (RIC) community and is generally accepting of those who are marginalized. They try to understand the experiences of those who are different from themselves.	Does the congregation know what a eunuch is? If so, what is their understanding of what it is and the significance to the story?	The "I Wonder / I Notice" exercise with my feedforward group via Zoom (with follow-up questions after if necessary).	There was understanding of what a eunuch physically was. However, there weren't really any wonderings or noticings about what the significance was of being a eunuch and how that affected his identity. There were a lot of questions about his religious identity but not so much about the way being a eunuch shaped his experience in the world.

K	W	H	L
2 The congregation is an RIC congregation and focusing on antiracism during the month of April (in part because Extraordinary Lutheran Ministries just added that RIC congregations must have an antiracism focus).	Does the congregation think the fact that the eunuch is Ethiopian is significant? If so, what significance do they find?	The "I Wonder / I Notice" exercise with my feedforward group via Zoom (with follow-up questions after if necessary).	There were a lot of wonderings about the eunuch's religious identity and the fact that he was coming from Ethiopia. The wonderings weren't so much about his "race" or culture so much as they were about religion and also his position in the Ethiopian court. They noticed that he was wealthy and that the journey was very far from Ethiopia. This made them wonder if he was sent by the queen for something else or if this was a personal trip, as that helps explain the motivation for the long, arduous journey.
3 The congregation is composed of people who have predominantly privileged identities and would most likely view themselves as those who are accepting others in.	Does the congregation imagine themselves more as Philip or the Ethiopian eunuch? Are they embracing somebody different, or are they somebody different? Or are they on the outside of it all (like the carriage driver)?	The literary exercise with my feedforward group via Zoom (with follow-up questions after if necessary).	Interestingly, nobody wrote from the perspective of Philip or the Ethiopian eunuch! I was really surprised. I imagined at least somebody would. Instead, two people wrote from the perspective of the Candace, two people wrote from the perspective of the chariot driver, and two people wrote from the perspective of the angel of the Lord. I was wondering if people would identify more with the evangelizers/people welcoming others in (Philip in this story) or more with the people on the outside being welcomed in (the Ethiopian eunuch), but they all chose somebody different. This makes me wonder if the people view themselves as outside of this dynamic? Which would be interesting to explore. Or if they were just curious about new perspectives into the story?

K	W	H	L
4 The congregation tends to think of themselves as helpers and those who give aid. I think they will think this story is evangelical or a happy story.	What do people think the vibe is? Is it pastoral? Is it bizarre? Is it comforting? Is it challenging?	Variation on the musical exercise with my feedforward group via Zoom. Ask, "What genre of music, or even better, what song would you say this story is and why?"	I was surprised by the genres/songs that people came up with. I was imagining an orchestral piece with very fast and dramatic violins, with twists and turns and drama. This story feels dramatic to me. It's a turning point. However, the responses I got were all about stories: (1) a ballad that tells a story where the eunuch goes off joyfully, (2) a big band piece that starts and builds and ends on a good note, (3) a song that builds and has an impact, like U2's "Beautiful Day," (4) the hymn "I Love to Tell the Story," (5) some sort of folk story with the tale ending in a good way, and (6) something that would be used at a celebration! An announcement of something good. It was really intriguing to me that the group really emphasized the joy of the eunuch at the end and that this was a story with a happy ending. That's a part of this story that I hadn't given much attention to. I notice that I feel suspicion at the eunuch's joy. The story is written from an insider perspective, so of course the outsider would be happy to be accepted in! But we don't actually get the outsider's perspective (in this story, the outsider isn't even named). So I think there's room to nuance the joy while still focusing on the story aspect of this Scripture.

K	W	H	L
5 This story is important for the formation of the early church, but I don't think the congregation will realize the larger/systemic significance of this story.	What do people think this story is for?	Ask, "If this story was a response to a question, what would the question be?"	The questions I got in response were the following: (1) Who is the good news intended for? Just Jews? Just residents of Israel? Just slaves and working folks? (2) What difference can one person make in someone's life? (3) How did Philip share the good news of Jesus's resurrection? (4) What happens when a curious soul is met with unexpected grace? and (5) People come into our lives for a reason. Some are to explain and guide, while others are for us to believe in. (This last one wasn't a question, but I think it gets at the gist of it.) This indicated to me that, mostly, everybody was viewing this as an individual story that only affected individual lives. I think this also might be reflected in the song choices that people made, where a lot of emphasis was put into the story and the joy of the one person. I think this is something I need to lean into in my sermon, and I should explain how this story can apply to our own individual lives while also pointing out the larger, systemic implications of this story (especially since it is most likely not a literal story but rather a story to explain the expansion of inclusion in the church). There's room in this story to be both small (as in affecting individuals) and big (as in affecting a larger sphere of society/community)!

KWHL Chart

Exegeting the congregation in light of Sunday's Scripture reading:

K	W	H	L
What do I KNOW about the congregation that might shape how they hear Sunday's Scripture readings?	What do I WANT to know about the congregation that might help me understand how they hear Sunday's Scripture readings?	HOW will I find out?	What did I LEARN about how the congregation engages this Scripture reading that might have an effect on the sermon?
1			
2			
3			
4			
5			

APPENDIX C
Sample Feedback Forms

Preacher _____ Respondent _____ Date _____

Recommended Sermon Title "_____"

1. **FUNCTION**
   a. What happened to you as you listened to the sermon?

   or

   b. This sermon _____ me. Please say
      more about your response.

2. **THEOLOGY:** According to this sermon, who is Jesus,
   and how is Jesus active in our lives today?

3. **GOOD NEWS:** In one sentence, identify the good news
   proclaimed in this sermon.

4. **SCRIPTURE:** What do you want to know more about?

5. **PROCLAMATION:** What would you tell another person
   about the sermon, and why?

6. **PRAYER:** For whom or for what does this sermon prompt
   you to pray?

Preacher _____ Respondent _____ Date _____

Recommended Sermon Title: "_____"

Respond to both questions, please:

1. What happened to you as you listened to this sermon?
   a. This sermon _____ me.

   or

   b. I was _____.

2. According to this sermon, who is God and how is God at work in the world?

Respond to two or three of the following questions (your choice):

1. What did you hear that you are eager to share with another person?

2. How might your actions change as a result of this sermon?

3. What in this sermon entices you to learn more about the biblical story?

4. For what and/or for whom does the sermon prompt you to pray?

Sermon Feedback Form

Your Name _____ Date of Sermon _____

Using a scale of 1–5 (with 1 = not at all descriptive and 5 = extremely descriptive), respond to each statement. (Feel free to explain further.) Thank you for your honest feedback!

1. The sermon was relevant to my life.
   1   2   3   4   5

2. The sermon reflected our discussions and what emerged through our collaborative work.
   1   2   3   4   5

3. I had some type of experience with God during this sermon.
   1   2   3   4   5

4. If I were to give this sermon a title it would be:

5. I appreciated _____ about the sermon.

6. If I were to change something about the sermon it would be:

7. According to this sermon, who is God?

8. Any additional comments, questions, concerns:

Please return your completed form to the pastor's mailbox in the office, hand it to an usher, or scan and email the completed form to the church office. Thank you so much for your honest comments and collaboration! Peace to you.

NAME: _____ **SERVICE DATE:** March 18, 2018[1]

SERVICE TIME: _____

GOSPEL AND FOCUS: John 12:20–33 + Human Trafficking

*Thanks for writing **something** in each box. Incomplete thoughts welcome!*

```
┌────────────────────────────────────────────────────┐
│         How was Christ preached in this sermon?      │
│                                                      │
│                                                      │
│                                                      │
│                                                      │
│                                                      │
│                                                      │
└────────────────────────────────────────────────────┘
```

```
┌────────────────────────────────────────────────────┐
│  What did you hear that you might share with another person?  │
│                                                      │
│                                                      │
│                                                      │
│                                                      │
│                                                      │
└────────────────────────────────────────────────────┘
```

Please return this form to Pastor Brenda or an usher. Bless you!

APPENDIX C

NAME: _____   SERVICE TIME: _____

HOLY GOSPEL: <u>Mark 1:1-8</u>   SERMON DATE: <u>10 December 2017</u>

In light of this sermon, **who** is God and **how** is God at work in the world?

What did you **hear** that you are eager to **share** with another person?

Please return this form to Pastor Brenda or an usher. Bless you!

NAME: _____   SERVICE TIME: _____

HOLY GOSPEL: <u>Mark 1:1-8</u>   SERMON DATE: <u>10 December 2017</u>

In light of this sermon, **who** is God and **how** is God at work in the world?

What did you **hear** that you are eager to **share** with another person?

Please return this form to Pastor Brenda or an usher. Bless you!

194

~ **worship notes** ~

name: _____

date: _____

today we are praying for:

musical moments

bits o' scripture

here's what I heard about Jesus

here's what I heard about the gospel

something new I learned today

questions I still have

_____
_____
_____

NOTES

Preface

1 Thank you to Jonathan Strandjord for this insight.
2 See Shauna K. Hannan, "Pass the Mic: Expanding Pulpit Privilege," *Currents in Theology and Mission* 47, no. 3 (Summer 2020): 31–34.

Introduction

1 Roger Alling and David J. Schlafer, *Preaching as the Art of Sacred Conversation*, Sermons That Work 6 (Harrisburg, PA: Morehouse, 1997), ix.
2 Barbara Brown Taylor, *The Preaching Life* (Lanham, MD: Rowman & Littlefield, 1993), 32.
3 Justo González and Catherine González, "The Neglected Interpreters," in *The Liberating Pulpit* (Nashville: Abingdon, 1994), 47–65.
4 Dietrich Ritschl, *A Theology of Proclamation* (Richmond, VA: WJKP, 1960), 15–16.
5 John McClure, *The Roundtable Pulpit: Where Leadership and Preaching Meet* (Nashville: Abingdon, 1995), 8.
6 Lucy Atkinson Rose, *Sharing the Word: Preaching in the Roundtable Church* (Louisville: WJKP, 1997), 121.
7 O. Wesley Allen Jr., *The Homiletic of All Believers: A Conversational Approach to Proclamation and Preaching* (Louisville: WJKP, 2005).
8 David Lose, *Preaching at the Crossroads: How the World—and Our Preaching—Is Changing* (Minneapolis: Fortress, 2013), 104–5.

9 Herman G. Stuempfle, *Preaching in the Witnessing Community* (Philadelphia: Fortress, 1973).

10 David Lose in the foreword to Patrick W. T. Johnson, *The Mission of Preaching: Equipping the Community for Faithful Witness* (Downers Grove, IL: InterVarsity, 2015), 10. Lose goes on to say, "Ultimately, the result of such preaching is that the appointed and authorized testimony of one (the 'preacher') equips, supports and authorizes the testimony of many (the 'congregation')."

Chapter 1

1 O. C. Edwards Jr., *A History of Preaching* (Nashville: Abingdon, 2004), 178.

2 Ronald J. Allen, "Preaching as Mutual Critical Correlation through Conversation," in *Purposes of Preaching*, ed. Jana Childers (St. Louis: Chalice, 2004), 1.

3 "La *predicación*, entonces, es una tarea interdisciplinaria donde el studio y la interpretación de la Biblia se encuentran con la teología sistemática, la historia de la iglesia, la educación Cristiana, el consejo pastoral y la oratoria. Así, pues, la predicaión es un ejercicio de integración teológica y pastoral." Pablo Jiménez, *Principios de Predicación* (Nashville: Abingdon, 2003), 19. Translation mine.

4 Taylor, *Preaching Life*, 32.

5 Stuempfle, *Preaching*, vii (italics added).

6 Mary Donovan Turner, "Disrupting a Ruptured World," in Childers, *Purposes of Preaching*, 135.

7 John A. Broadus, *On the Preparation and Delivery of Sermons*, rev. Jesse Burton Weatherspoon (New York: Harper & Bros., 1944), 157, quoted in Rose, *Sharing the Word*, 14.

8 Broadus, *On the Preparation*, 24, quoted in Rose, *Sharing the Word*, 14.

9 Rose, *Sharing the Word*, 37.

10 Robert H. Mounce, *The Essential Nature of New Testament Preaching* (Grand Rapids, MI: Eerdmans, 1960), 158, quoted in Rose, *Sharing the Word*, 38.

11 Clement Welsh, *Preaching in a New Key: Studies in the Psychology of Thinking and Listening* (Philadelphia: Pilgrim, 1974), 103, quoted in Rose, *Sharing the Word*, 38.

12 W. Norman Pittenger in *Proclaiming Christ Today* (Greenwich, CO: Seabury, 1962), referenced by Rose, *Sharing the Word*, 45.

13 Alvin J. Porteous, *Preaching to Suburban Captives* (Valley Forge, PA: Judson, 1979), 34, quoted in Rose, *Sharing the Word*, 53.

14 Justo González and Catherine González, *Liberation Preaching: The Pulpit and the Oppressed* (Nashville: Abingdon, 1980), 15, quoted in Rose, *Sharing the Word*, 53.

15 Rose, *Sharing the Word*, 36.

16 González and González, *Liberation Preaching*, 16–19, quoted in Rose, *Sharing the Word*, 53.

17 I recommend actually facilitating a Bible study in which small groups discuss how and why they would articulate the good news as they do in these settings.

18 Pablo Jiménez, "The Laborers of the Vineyard (Matthew 20:1–16): A Hispanic Homiletical Reading," *Journal for Preachers* 21, no. 1 (Advent 1997): 35–40; and Eugene Lowry, "Who Could Ask for Anything More?," in *How to Preach a Parable: Designs for Narrative Sermons* (Nashville: Abingdon, 1989), 115–20.

19 Jiménez, "Laborers," 36.

20 Jiménez, 39.

21 Jiménez, 37.

22 Robert W. Duke, *The Sermon as God's Word*, ed. William D. Thompson (Nashville: Abingdon, 1980), 97, quoted in Rose, *Sharing the Word*, 66.

23 Claude H. Thompson, *Theology of the Kerygma: A Study in Primitive Preaching* (Englewood Cliffs, NJ: Prentice-Hall, 1962), 25, quoted in Rose, *Sharing the Word*, 104.

24 Rose, *Sharing the Word*, 103.

25 For example, "What might be liberating to one set of worshipers, say, men, might be oppressive to another, say, women." William A. Beardslee et al., *Biblical Preaching on the Death of Jesus* (Nashville: Abingdon, 1989), 36, 134, as referenced by Rose, *Sharing the Word*, 101.

26 Rose, *Sharing the Word*, 59.

27 Fred Craddock, *As One without Authority*, 3rd ed. (Nashville: Abingdon, 1978), 55, quoted in Rose, *Sharing the Word*, 61.

28 Paul Scott Wilson, *Imaginations of the Heart: New Understandings in Preaching* (Nashville: Abingdon, 1988), 29.

29 Rose, *Sharing the Word*, 61.

30 Rose, 66.

31 Rose, 77.

32 Christine's Smith's work in *Weaving the Sermon* (Louisville: WJKP, 1989), 48, quoted in Rose, *Sharing the Word*, 89.

33 Rose, *Sharing the Word*, 98.

34 Rose, 90.

35 Rose says that "[Robert Browne] proposes that preaching's aim is to nurture a process whereby worshipers take responsibility for making sense of their own lives." See Robert E. C. Browne, *The Ministry of the Word* (London: SCM, 1958), quoted in Rose, *Sharing the Word*, 92.

36 Rose, *Sharing the Word*, 95.

37 Rose, 98.

38 Luke 4:18–19 NIV. See also Isa 61:1–2; 58:6.

Chapter 2

1 Matthew Skinner, *Intrusive God, Disruptive Gospel: Encountering the Divine in the Book of Acts* (Grand Rapids, MI: Brazos, 2015), 93.

2 *Euangelizomenōn* (Luke 4:43; Acts 5:42; Eph 2:17).

3 *Kerusso* (Mark 1:14; Luke 4:44; Acts 8:5; 1 Cor 1:23).

4 *Martureo* (John 15:27; Acts 26:22; 1 John 1:2).

5 Elizabeth Achtemeier, *Creative Preaching* (Nashville: Abingdon, 1980), 23–24.

6 Achtemeier, 21.

7 Martin Luther, "First Sunday in Advent" (1522 sermon on Matthew 21:1–9), lutherdansk.dk, accessed June 15, 2021, http://www.lutherdansk.dk/Web-advent%20engelsk-KP/Adventpostillen.htm.

8 Martin Luther, "A Brief Introduction on What to Look for and Expect in the Gospels," in *Luther's Works: Word and Sacrament I*, ed., J. J. Pelikan, H. C. Oswald, and H. T. Lehmann (Philadelphia: Fortress, 1955–76; hereafter cited as LW), 35:123.

9 Charles L. Bartow, *God's Human Speech: A Practical Theology of Proclamation* (Grand Rapids, MI: Eerdmans, 1997), 4.

10 Achtemeier, *Creative Preaching*, 46.

11 Other denominations might grapple similarly—for example, Reformed churches with John Calvin, the United Methodist Church with John Wesley, and the Roman Catholic Church with various papal pronouncements.

12 LW 44:179. Again, Luther claimed, "When Christ is preached, Christ is preaching."

13 Martin Luther, Weimarer Ausgabe (hereafter cited as WA) 10, III, 260; 17, II, 174, as cited in Paul Althaus, *The Theology of Martin Luther* (Philadelphia: Fortress Press, 1966), 39.

14 LW 51, 76; and WA 10, III, 15.

15 WA 17, II, 179.

16 *Augsburg Confession*, Article V (Concerning the Office of Preaching).

17 *Augsburg Confession*, Article V.

18 ELCA Constitution, 1995, 4.02.d.

19 ELCA Constitution, 1995, 4.02.a.

20 ELCA Constitution, 1995, S14.12, 193.

21 ELCA Constitution, 1995, S14.32, 197.

22 *The Use of the Means of Grace: A Statement on the Practice of Word and Sacrament* (Chicago: Evangelical Lutheran Church in America, 1997). This statement is reprinted as the appendix in ELCA, *Principles for Worship* (Chicago: Evangelical Lutheran Church in America, 2002), 97–143, https://download.elca.org/ELCA%20Resource%20Repository/Principles_for_Worship.pdf?_ga=2.265972425.734543659.1610231027-1000883088.1610053464. *The Use of the Means of Grace* was adopted by the Fifth Biennial Churchwide Assembly of the ELCA, August 19, 1997, by a vote of 857 in favor, 44 against, for guidance and practice. Note that in the ELCA, assembly is laypeople and clergy.

23 ELCA, *Use of the Means of Grace.*

24 ELCA, *Principles for Worship*, vi.

25 ELCA, vi.

26 ELCA, viii.

27 ELCA, 49.

28 ELCA, 52.

29 ELCA, 59.

30 ELCA, 66.

31 For example, in the Roman Catholic Church, one might review documents such as *Compendium: Catechism of the Roman Catholic Church* (Washington, DC: United States Conference of Catholic Bishops, 2006); Pope Francis, *The Joy of the Gospel: Evangelii Gaudium* (Washington, DC: United States Conference of Catholic Bishops, 2013); and *Fulfilled in Your Hearing: The Homily in the Sunday Assembly* (Washington, DC: United States Conference of Catholic Bishops, 1982). In the Anglican tradition, see *The Book of Common Prayer and Administration of the Sacraments and Other Rites and Ceremonies of the Church: Together with the Psalter or Psalms of David according to the Use of the Episcopal Church* (New York: Seabury, 1979), 874–75. In the Reformed traditions, see "The Second Helvetic Confessions" and "The Preaching of the Word of God Is the Word of God," in *The Book of Confessions* (Louisville: Presbyterian Church [US], 1994), C5.004, 55–56. The tagline of the United Church of Christ, "God is still speaking," is instructive.

Chapter 3

1 Accompaniment is a scriptural and practical way of understanding mission that has been articulated in the past few decades in dialogue between churches in the "Global North" (the churches that historically sent missionaries) and churches in the "Global South" (churches in Asia, Africa, and Latin America that historically received missionaries). Today, there are more Christians in the Global South than in the Global North: "It's a different world than

that of the earliest missionaries, and our understanding of and living out mission must respond." "Accompaniment," 2013 ELCA Glocal Mission Gathering, http://download.elca.org/ELCA%20Resource%20Repository/Accompaniment_(full).pdf.

2 Skinner, *Intrusive God*, 66. See also Ernesto Cardenal, *The Gospel in Solentiname* (Maryknoll, NY: Orbis, 2010).

3 Kyle Oliver, "Listening Sessions: Fourteen Colleagues on Leadership, Formation, and the Future of the Church," *Crossings*, Fall 2020, 4–11.

4 Some seminaries have even integrated community organizing courses into the curriculum. The two examples I am most familiar with are both member schools of the Graduate Theological Union (Berkeley, CA): Pacific Lutheran Theological Seminary and Church Divinity School of the Pacific.

5 Barack Obama, *A Promised Land* (New York: Random House, 2020), 14.

6 Obama, 18. For additional principles, see Chuck Warpehoski, "7 Principles of Community Organizing," Interfaith Council for Peace and Justice, accessed June 15, 2021, http://www.icpj.org/blog/wp-content/uploads/2016/07/7-Principles-of-Community-Organizing.pdf.

7 See "About the Gamaliel Religious Leaders Caucus," Gamaliel, accessed June 15, 2021, https://gamaliel.org/our-work/religious-leaders-caucus/.

8 See José David Rodriguez and Loida I. Martell-Otero, eds., *Teología en Conjunto: A Collaborative Hispanic Protestant Theology* (Louisville: WJKP, 1997).

9 Michael Allaby, *A Guide to Gaia: A Survey of the New Science of Our Living Earth* (New York: E. P. Dutton, 1989), 109, quoted in Chuck Champlin, *Think like a Molecule: Finding Inspiration in Connection and Collaboration* (Bloomington, IN: Archway, 2018), 76.

10 Ferris Jabr, "The Social Life of Forests," *New York Times Magazine*, December 2, 2020, https://www.nytimes.com/interactive/2020/12/02/magazine/tree-communication-mycorrhiza.html. Simard inspired the central character, botanist Patricia Westerford, in Richard Powers's 2019 Pulitzer Prize–winning novel, *The Overstory* (New York: W. W. Norton, 2018).

11 Rose, *Sharing the Word*, 145. Footnote 3 of chap. 5 mentions Browne Barr's book *High Flying Geese: Unexpected Reflections on the Church and Its Ministry* (New York: Seabury, 1983) as well as James Belasco and Ralph Stayer's leadership book *Flight of the Buffalo: Soaring to Excellence, Learning to Let Employees Lead* (New York: Warner, 1993).

12 Harvey Schachter, "What Workplaces Need to Learn from Bees," *Globe and Mail*, July 7, 2013, https://www.theglobeandmail.com/report-on-business/careers/management/what-workplaces-need-to-learn-from-bees/article13036442/.

13 David Zinger, "Waggle: 39 Ways to Improve Human Organizations, Work and Engagement," davidzinger.com, May 20, 2013, https://www.davidzinger.com/wp-content/uploads/Waggle-by-David-Zinger.pdf. The author, a Winnipeg-based consultant and host of the 5,900-member Employee Engagement Network, offers three directions for "collaborating incessantly": "1. Use social media tools to spread and speed collaboration. If you want everyone on the same page give them an opportunity to write on that page. Instead of going on a retreat for strategy development connect with all employees to craft strategy. 2. Transform hero leaders into hosts and ensure collaboration by following this dictum of collaborative work: never do anything about me without me. 3. Ask yourself: Who are we missing rather than what are we missing for successful collaboration?"

14 Thomas D. Seeley, *Honeybee Democracy* (Princeton, NJ: Princeton University Press, 2010), 222, quoted in Zinger, "Waggle."

15 Albert Einstein was onto something when he said, "If the bee disappeared off the surface of the globe, then man would have only four years of life left. No more bees, no more pollination, no more plants, no more animals, no more man." Both Packer and Einstein are quoted in Tucson Bee Collective (website), accessed June 15, 2021, https://www.tucsonbeecollaborative.com/.

16 "Introduction," Biomimicry Toolbox, accessed June 15, 2021, https://toolbox.biomimicry.org/introduction/.

17 Champlin, *Think like a Molecule*, 27–28. We could go on and on as we learn more about nature's ecosystems.

18 Q&A with Amy Banks, MD, director of advanced training at the Jean Baker Miller Training Institute at the Wellesley Centers for Women, instructor of psychiatry at Harvard Medical School, coeditor of *The Complete Guide to Mental Health for Women*, and author of *Post-traumatic Stress Disorder: Relationships and Brain Chemistry*. See Wellesley Centers for Women, "Humans Are Hardwired for Connection? Neurobiology 101 for Parents, Educators, Practitioners, and the General Public," September 15, 2010, https://www.wcwonline.org/2010/humans-are-hardwired-for-connection-neurobiology-101-for-parents-educators-practitioners-and-the-general-public.

19 "Definition: Collaborative Awareness," Center for Collaborative Awareness, August 26, 2019, https://www.collaborativeawareness.com/post/definition-collaborative-awareness.

20 Matthew D. Lieberman, *Social: Why Our Brains Are Wired to Connect* (New York: Crown, 2013), 41. In 1943, Abraham Maslow, a famous New England psychologist, published a paper in a prestigious journal describing a hierarchy of needs in humans. The pyramid shows physiological needs at the bottom as foundational. As one moves up the pyramid, this is followed by safety, social, esteem, and self-actualization.

21 Lieberman, 22.

22 Lieberman, 43.

23 Lieberman, 300.

24 Wellesley Centers for Women, "Humans Are Hardwired." Banks says, "What [researchers] found was the area that lit up in the brain for that kind of social rejection—the anterior cingulate—was the exact same area that lights up for the distress of physical pain."

25 Saint Augustine, "Book IV," in *De Doctrina Christiana*, trans. D. W. Robertson (Indianapolis: Bobbs-Merrill, 1958).

26 Emily Campbell, "Six Surprising Benefits of Curiosity," *Greater Good Magazine*, September 24, 2015, https://greatergood.berkeley.edu/article/item/six_surprising_benefits_of_curiosity. It's worth our time considering this question, since developing a curiosity of how the world works has health benefits for humans. Curiosity often leads to

discovering new things, which leads to the brain's release of natural "feel-good chemicals" such as dopamine.

27 Jill Suttie, "Why Are We So Wired to Connect?," *Greater Good Magazine*, December 2, 2013, https://greatergood.berkeley.edu/article/item/why_are_we_so_wired_to_connect.

28 Lieberman, *Social*, 294–95. "People who were learning to juggle for a few short months came to have greater cortical thickness in brain regions involved in motion perception, an effect that lasted long after the individuals ceased juggling."

29 Peter C. Brown et al., *Make It Stick: The Science of Successful Learning* (Cambridge, MA: Belknap, 2014), 3–4. John Dewey had already noticed these phenomena. Dewey was an American public intellectual in the late nineteen to early twentieth century whose education reforms continue to have an impact on education today. His idea of progressive education utilized hands-on learning—that is, "learning by doing."

30 James Lang, "Distracted Minds: Your Classroom Can Be a Retreat in Dark Times," *Chronicle of Higher Education*, January 15, 2021, https://www.chronicle.com/article/distracted-minds-your-classroom-can-be-a-retreat-in-dark-times. Lang refers to Mihaly Csikszentmihalyi's work in his book *Flow: The Psychology of Optimal Experience* (New York: Harper Perennial, 1990).

31 Gareth Cook, "Why We Are Wired to Connect," *Scientific American*, October 22, 2013, https://www.scientificamerican.com/article/why-we-are-wired-to-connect/.

32 R. T. Johnson and D. W. Johnson, "Action Research: Cooperative Learning in the Science Classroom," *Science and Children* 24, no. 2 (1986): 31–32.

33 Suttie, "Wired to Connect?"

34 Joost M. Vervoort, Kasper Kok, Ron van Lammeren, and A. Veldkamp, "Stepping into Futures: Exploring the Potential of Interactive Media for Participatory Scenarios on Social-Ecological Systems," *Futures* 42, no. 6 (August 2010): 604–16. https://doi.org/10.1016/j.futures.2010.04.031.

35 Henry Jenkins et al., *Confronting the Challenges of Participatory Culture: Media Education for the 21st Century* (Cambridge, MA: MIT, 2009), http://www.newmedialiteracies.org/wp-content/uploads/pdfs/NMLWhitePaper.pdf. Jenkins is the director of the Comparative Media Studies Program at MIT. Henry Jenkins, *Confronting the Challenges of Participatory Culture: Media Education for the 21st Century* (Chicago: MacArthur Foundation, 2006), 3.

36 Jenkins, 7.

37 Wikipedia, s.v. "Wikinomics," last modified April 14, 2021, 9:47, https://en.wikipedia.org/wiki/Wikinomics. The entry refers to the work of Don Tapscott and Anthony D. Williams in their book *Wikinomics: How Mass Collaboration Changes Everything* (New York: Portfolio, 2006). It was only one year prior to the publication of this book that the term *crowdsourcing* was coined by Jeff Howe and Mark Robinson, editors of *Wired* magazine, to describe how businesses were using the internet to "outsource work to the crowd." This phrase led to the portmanteau *crowdsourcing*.

38 I am aware that "preaching" and "performance" are often considered to be at odds, since preaching is not solely for entertainment or to heighten performers' egos (to be sure, performers in a variety of arts, including film, expect their performances to move beyond these two outcomes as well). However, preaching is a performance in that it "completes, carries out, accomplishes" something its Old French etymology suggests (*parfournir*). Indeed, preaching brings an experience or a text to life.

39 *Hearer* is assumed to be passive and *listener* active. Many homiletical theorists tend not to use the word *audience* because it could assume passivity even though communication theorists have long argued there is no such thing.

40 Robin Meyers quotes Schramm in *With Ears to Hear: Preaching as Self-Persuasion* (Eugene, OR: Wipf & Stock, 1989), 27.

41 One might say then that while people evaluate sermons, they are also responsible for evaluating their own reactions to sermons.

42 Baz Kershaw, *The Politics of Performance: Radical Theatre as Cultural Intervention* (London: Routledge, 1992), 16–17.

43 While the theatre in the round was common in ancient Greco-Roman theatre, it had fallen out of favor until the twentieth century.

44 Doug Paterson, "A Brief Biography of Augusto Boal," Pedagogy and Theatre of the Oppressed, accessed March 30, 2021, https://ptoweb .org/aboutpto/a-brief-biography-of-augusto-boal/.

45 For more information, see the website for Theatre of the Oppressed NYC, https://www.tonyc.nyc. If one were to respect the Latinate etymology of the word *performance* (that is, *per-form* = through form), Theatre of the Oppressed might be considered the purist of performances as it intends to carry through to completion in real life what was rehearsed on the stage.

46 Meyers, *With Ears to Hear*, 29.

47 For more on the connection between preaching and theatre, see Jana Childers, *Performing the Word: Preaching as Theatre* (Nashville: Abingdon, 1998); and Jana Childers and Clayton J. Schmit, eds., *Performance in Preaching: Bringing the Sermon to Life* (Grand Rapids, MI: Baker Academic, 2008).

48 Gemma Joyce, "Crowdsourcing a Review of *Black Mirror: Bandersnatch*," Brandwatch, January 2, 2019, https://www.brandwatch.com/ blog/react-black-mirror-bandersnatch-review/.

49 William D. Romanowski, *Cinematic Faith: A Christian Perspective on Movies and Meaning* (Grand Rapids, MI: Baker Academic, 2019), 55.

50 "The Role of Film Teams," Impact Field Guide & Toolkit, Doc Society, accessed June 15, 2021, https://impactguide.org/impact-in-action/the -role-of-film-teams/. See also Jackson DeMos, "Research Study Finds That a Film Can Have a Measurable Impact on Audience Behavior," USC Annenberg School for Communication and Journalism, February 22, 2012, https://annenberg.usc.edu/news/centers/research-study -finds-film-can-have-measurable-impact-audience-behavior.

51 Dave McNary, "Netflix Teams with Ron Howard and Brian Grazer's Imagine Impact to Develop Films from Rising Screenwriters," *Variety*, June 17, 2020, https://variety.com/2020/film/news/netflix-ron -howard-brian-grazer-imagine-1234637665/#!.

52 See Shauna Hannan, "Impact Teams," in "'What Preachers Can Learn from Filmmakers,'" part 2 (of 4), "Impact Teams," Wabash Center for Teaching and Learning in Theology and Religion, 2019–20, https://www.wabashcenter.wabash.edu/2020/02/what-preachers -can-learn-from-filmmakers-part-2-of-4-impact-teams/.

Chapter 4

1 Rose, *Sharing the Word*, 39.

2 Martin Marty, *The Word: People Participating in Preaching* (Philadelphia: Fortress, 1984), 15, 19.

3 Thomas G. Long, *The Witness of Preaching*, 3rd ed. (Louisville: WJKP, 2016), 265.

4 See, for example, Cleophus J. LaRue, *Power in the Pulpit: How America's Most Effective Black Preachers Prepare Their Sermons* (Louisville: WJKP, 2009); and Jana Childers, *Birthing the Sermon: Women Preachers on the Creative Process* (St. Louis: Chalice, 2001).

5 Fred Craddock, *Preaching* (Nashville: Abingdon, 1985), 99.

6 James Nieman, *Knowing the Context: Frames, Tools, and Signs for Preaching* (Minneapolis: Fortress, 2008), 7.

7 Stephen Farris, "Exegesis of the Congregation," in *New Interpreter's Handbook of Preaching*, ed. Paul Scott Wilson (Nashville: Abingdon, 2008), 267.

8 Leonora Tubbs Tisdale's book *Preaching as Local Theology and Folk Art* (Minneapolis: Fortress, 1997) is a great place to start.

9 Rose, *Sharing the Word*, 128.

10 Mary Hulst, "Introduction: Social Location," in Wilson, *New Interpreter's Handbook of Preaching*, 253.

11 Nieman, *Knowing the Context*, 9.

12 Leander Keck, *The Bible in the Pulpit: The Renewal of Biblical Preaching* (Nashville: Abingdon, 1978), 59.

13 Walter Brueggemann, "The Social Nature of the Biblical Text for Preaching," in *Preaching as a Social Act: Theology and Practice*, ed. Arthur Van Seters (Nashville: Abingdon, 1988), 131, quoted in Rose, *Sharing the Word*, 79.

14 Elisabeth Schüssler Fiorenza, response in *A New Look at Preaching*, ed. John Burke (Wilmington, DE: Good News Studies, 1983), 44, quoted in Rose, *Sharing the Word*, 79.

15 Gardner Taylor, "Shaping Sermons by the Shape of Text and Preacher," in *Preaching Biblically*, ed. Don Wardlaw (Philadelphia: Westminster, 1983), 138, quoted in Rose, *Sharing the Word*, 80.

16 Rose, *Sharing the Word*, 55.

17 Rose, 56.

18 A simple internet search will yield numerous uses and examples.

19 González and González, *Liberation Preaching*, 19, 76. The not-to-be-missed point here is the importance of broadening one's perspective. Schüssler Fiorenza insists that "it is only by taking seriously those interpretations that conflict with one's own theological and social presuppositions and conditions that the homilist is capable of broadening out the experiential and interpretative basis of proclamation." Schüssler Fiorenza, response in *A New Look*, 52.

20 González and González, "Neglected Interpreters," 47–50. It is worth revisiting Dietrich Ritchl's comment noted above: "Part of the cruelty (which we ourselves have created) of our Church is that minister and congregation are separated in such a way the preacher is alone and isolated with [the] preaching task."

21 Greg Carey, *Using Our Outside Voice: Public Biblical Interpretation* (Minneapolis: Fortress, 2020), 5.

22 I hope one's work with commentaries, while a vital part of the process, is saved as a later step so as not to shortcut the wisdom and creativity of you and your community. See Shauna Hannan, "Using Commentaries Effectively and Faithfully," Working Preacher, April 5, 2019, https://www.workingpreacher.org/sermon-development/using-commentaries-effectively-and-faithfully.

23 Elizabeth Liebert, "Academic Life and Scholarship as Spiritual Practice," *Berkeley Journal of Religion and Theology* 3, no. 1 (2017): 12–28.

24 Liebert, 13.

25 Elizabeth Liebert, "Academic Life and Scholarship as Spiritual Practice," Graduate Theological Union, November 15, 2017, https://www.gtu.edu/news/academic-life-and-scholarship-spiritual-practice.

26 Long, *Witness of Preaching*, 92.

27 Long, 101.

28 See Long's list in *Witness of Preaching*, 96–101.

29 "The Art of Wondering," Godly Play UK, accessed June 15, 2021, https://www.godlyplay.uk/wp-content/uploads/2013/05/The-Art -of-Wondering.pdf. The website also says about wondering that it is "rather like the difference between a pianist who can play all the right notes, and the artist who really conveys the music from a place deep within them."

30 "Art of Wondering."

31 For a more detailed description, see Tom S. Long, "Freeze Frame: Dramatic Scripture Telling Using Tableaux," *Reformed Worship* 75 (March 2005), https://www.reformedworship.org/article/march-2005/freeze -frame-dramatic-scripture-telling-using-tableaux.

32 Pamela Ann Moeller, *Kinesthetic Homiletic: Embodying Gospel in Preaching* (Minneapolis: Fortress, 1993), 3.

33 Specifically related to preaching controversial issues, see Leah Schade, *Preaching in the Purple Zone: Ministry in the Red-Blue Divide* (Lanham, MD: Rowman & Littlefield, 2019).

Chapter 5

1 I can imagine an even more extreme option—that is, abdicating all responsibility for the preaching ministry by handing it over to anyone who wants to pick it up. However, I'm assuming we're working within the bounds of a called pastor fulfilling one's vow to steward the pulpit in some way so that faithful proclamation happens.

2 I have no reason to doubt the experience of those who say the Q&A option is effective, but that is not my proposal. I can imagine, and give an example below, of "Q&A" as one move of many within a sermon. I have experimented with a variation on the dialogue sermon. See Shauna K. Hannan, "When Scripture Speaks Out of Both Sides of Its Mouth: Dueling Preachers on a Faithful Food Ethic," *Word and World* 33, no. 4 (October 1, 2013): 399–405.

3 HyeRan Kim-Cragg, *Postcolonial Preaching* (Lanham, MD: Lexington, 2021), 90. I appreciate Kim-Cragg's reminder that "knowledge is perspectival and perspectives are power-laden" (110).

4 "Sermon—8 Dec 2019," Grace Lutheran Church Wenatchee, December 10, 2019, YouTube video, https://youtu.be/ji9sp_Gomv8.

5 Email communication with M. Baumgartner.

6 Leonora Tubbs Tisdale, *Prophetic Preaching: A Pastoral Approach* (Louisville: WJKP, 2010), 55–56.

7 Tisdale, 98.

8 Tisdale, 98.

9 James Aalgaard, "Peace Be Still—Mark 4:35–41—Pastor James Aalgaard," Grace Lutheran Church Wenatchee, December 8, 2019, YouTube video, https://youtu.be/Hoc7RCSw6Nk.

10 ZamaMdoda, "'Tell Them about the Dream, Martin!' Mahalia Jackson," Afropunk, January 21, 2019, https://afropunk.com/2019/01/tell-them-about-the-dream-martin-mahalia-jackson/.

11 Stuart Strachan Jr., "Tell Them about the Dream Martin!," *Pastor's Workshop* (blog), January 20, 2020, https://thepastorsworkshop.com/tell-them-about-the-dream-martin/.

12 Reuel Howe, *The Miracle of Dialogue* (New York: Seabury, 1965), 40–41.

13 Howe, 43. Throughout the book, Howe answers his own question, "Why should [the laity] be involved in the church's preaching?"

14 Howe, 40–41.

15 Teresa Fry Brown, *Delivering the Sermon: Voice, Body, and Animation in Proclamation* (Minneapolis: Fortress, 2008), 19. Reflecting on Fry-Brown's words, HyeRan Kim-Cragg says, "The body language of the congregation is relational and responsive; it performs a kind of theological language in conversation with the preacher." Kim-Cragg, *Postcolonial Preaching*, 88–89.

16 Podcasts, by the way, are a great example of how much more engaging it is when the host embeds actual voices of other people into the show as opposed to simply reading a quote from that other person.

17 Moeller, *Kinesthetic Homiletic*, 5. I am reminded of Psalm 19: "The heavens are telling the glory of God; and the firmament proclaims his

handiwork. Day to day pours forth speech, and night to night declares knowledge. There is no speech, nor are there words; their voice is not heard; yet their voice goes out through all the earth, and their words to the end of the world" (vv. 1–4).

18 Moeller, 3.

19 Kim-Cragg, *Postcolonial Preaching*, 89.

20 Email correspondence with Holmerud.

21 The formatting reflects the sermon script used. Instead of neatly organized paragraphing (which is a format meant for readers and unfortunately results in preachers simply reading something from the paper), a sermon script should be formatted to cue the preacher for an effective delivery. In homiletics, we refer to this as "writing for the ear." Although its presentation here is for readers, the script has not been altered from its original format so as not to reinforce the assumption that a sermon script should reflect the formatting of a written essay.

22 Email correspondence with Baumgartner.

23 Email correspondence with Hamill.

24 Thomas H. Troeger and H. Edward Everding Jr., eds., *So That All Might Know: Preaching That Engages the Whole Congregation* (Nashville: Abingdon, 2008), 7.

25 Rose, *Sharing the Word*, 125.

26 John McClure, *Other-Wise Preaching: A Postmodern Ethic for Homiletics* (St. Louis: Chalice, 2001), 7.

27 Elisabeth Schüssler Fiorenza goes so far as to propose that "the clergy should relinquish their monopoly of the pulpit, since the right to preach derives from baptism and from each believer's experience of God." Rose, *Sharing the Word*, 97, refers to Elisabeth Schüssler Fiorenza in Burke, *New Look at Preaching*, 48, 55.

28 Lucy Atkinson Rose asks, "Who exercises control over the interpretive process and therefore over preaching's content?" (Rose, *Sharing the Word*, 106).

29 Rose, 97.

30 While I think it is faithful and beneficial occasionally to have an "outside voice," I've come to believe there is more impact when people

within a community are equipped to preach. I have argued elsewhere for a thoroughgoing movement toward lay preaching. See Shauna Hannan, "That All Might Proclaim: Continuing Luther's Legacy of Access," *Dialog: A Journal of Theology* 56, no. 2 (June 2017): 169–75.

31 In addition, it must be said that bad theology can and does come from ordained ministers, which for me is exponentially detrimental when assumed to be the *only* theology. Wes Allen says, "Having a Master of Divinity does not mean one has truly mastered divinity" (Allen, *Homiletic of All Believers*, 20). I appreciate Rose's litmus test: "For me, the critical issue in conversational preaching is not whether preaching meets some absolute standard of orthodoxy but whether sermonic interpretations, proposals and wagers serve to foster all the central conversations of the church as the people of God, whether they upbuild the communities of faith in their local and global configurations (see 1 Cor 14:12), and whether they respect and invite the voices of the silenced, the disenfranchised, the poor, and women" (Rose, *Sharing the Word*, 106).

32 Not even an open-source service like Wikipedia is "anything goes." A variety of people are assigned to monitor content (have you read Wikipedia's policy on "edit warring"?).

33 Email correspondence with Aalgaard.

34 Email correspondence with Aalgaard.

35 Email correspondence with Aalgaard.

36 Others' writings have helped to develop a homiletic that leaves room for listeners to come to their own conclusions, but they have done so in ways that do not require the active participation that this book proposes. See Craddock, *One without Authority*; and Eugene Lowry, *The Homiletical Plot*, rev. ed. (Louisville: WJKP, 2001).

37 For an example of engaging different locations without technology, see Lisa Dahill, "Indoors, Outdoors: Praying with the Earth," in *Eco-Lutheranism: Lutheran Perspectives on Ecology*, ed. Karla G. Bohmbach and Shauna K. Hannan (Minneapolis: Lutheran University Press, 2013), 113–24.

38 Hallie Parkins, "Worship Service September 13th," St. Mark's Lutheran Church by the Narrows, September 13, 2020, Facebook video, https://www.facebook.com/115652548458311/videos/3464609160271936 (the sermon begins at 13:50).

39 Hallie Parkins, "Worship Service February 14th, 2021," St. Mark's Lutheran Church by the Narrows, February 14, 2021, Facebook video, https://www.facebook.com/115652548458311/videos/238966234326286.

40 Coined by Alvin Toffler in his book *The Third Wave* (New York: Bantam, 1984). Wikipedia, s.v. "Prosumer," last modified June 11, 2021, 6:34, https://en.wikipedia.org/wiki/Prosumer. For a creative example of using digital culture for preaching, see John McClure, *Mashup Religion: Pop Music and Theological Invention* (Waco, TX: Baylor University Press, 2011). McClure offers an intriguing homiletical proposal when he refers to "mashup religion" as a kind of a "musical pastiche." "Mashup" artists, such as popular music producers, "stretch the boundaries of creativity by freely intermingling old sounds and melodies with the newest technologies." McClure highlights two of the five classical canons of rhetoric, *inventio* and *disposition*: (1) *inventio*, or what to say (think of content as an invention that doesn't require a patent), and (2) the arrangement of that content, called *dispositio*. For mashup artists, "invention is juxtaposing sounds to make something new" in a kind of "stylistic morphing." McClure's work makes me think of the sermon-crafting process as curating an experience of the living word of God.

Chapter 6

1 I was fascinated to discover that "response times after sermons were widespread in the churches of New England during the early seventeenth century." Rose, *Sharing the Word*, 130, refers to Doug Adams's work, *Meeting House to Camp Meeting: Toward a History of American Free Church Worship from 1620 to 1835* (Saratoga, CA: Modern Liturgy Resource Publication, 1981).

2 The summary of Lori Carrell's book, *The Great American Sermon Survey* (Wheaton, IL: Mainstay Church Resources, 2000), is illustrative: "'Good sermon.' This comment and a handshake—that's about as much as most listeners are willing to provide to their preachers after a sermon. In fact, a vast majority of listeners and preachers never talk to each other about sermons. In some ways, this is the forbidden topic!"

3 See, for example, Allen, *Homiletic of All Believers*, 5.

4 Howe, *Miracle of Dialogue*, 32.

5 Browne, *Ministry of the Word*, 25, quoted in Rose, *Sharing the Word*, 91. Note that Browne's work was published prepostmodernism.

6 Rose, *Sharing the Word*, 90.

7 Rose, 91.

8 Rose, 89, 91.

9 Rose, 98.

10 The director of the study, Ron Allen, summarizes the study in "Listening to Listeners: Five Years Later," *Homiletic* 34, no. 2 (2009): 4–17, https://ejournals.library.vanderbilt.edu/index.php/homiletic/article/view/3376. This article references two other resources derived from this study: Ronald J. Allen, "The Turn to the Listener: A Selective Review of a Recent Trend in Preaching," *Encounter* 64, no. 2 (2003): 167–96; and Margaret Moers Wenig, "Bringing Congregants into the Classroom: Learning from the Listeners," *Papers of the Annual Meeting of the Academy of Homiletics*, 36th Meeting, 138–52. Other works include Clifton F. Guthrie, "Quantitative Empirical Studies in Preaching: A Review of Methods and Findings," *Journal of Communication and Religion* 30, no. 1 (March 2007): 65–117; and Eric Reed, "The Preaching Report Card: Today's Listeners Grade Pastors on What They Hear from the Pulpit," *Leadership* 20 (Summer 1999): 84.

11 Allen, "Turn to the Listener," 193.

12 Carrell, *Great American Sermon Survey*, 150–54.

13 Rose, *Sharing the Word*, 100.

14 M. J. Haemig, "Reclaiming the Empowerment of Ordinary People," in *The Forgotten Luther II*, ed. Ryan P. Cumming (Minneapolis: Fortress, 2019), 41–54, quote on 47.

15 M. J. Haemig, "Laypeople as Overseers of the Faith," *Trinity Seminary Review* 27 (2006): 21–27, 24 is quoted here. Haemig is quoting Luther from his treatises: *To the Christian Nobility of the German Nation* (1520) and *Concerning the Ministry* (1523).

16 Haemig, "Reclaiming," 44.

17 Haemig, 44.

18 A number of churches have begun their own versions of getting back to the basics regarding Scripture. For example, the ELCA's Book of Faith Initiative seeks to "increase biblical literacy and fluency for the sake of the world." See Book of Faith (homepage), https://www.bookoffaith .org. The Episcopal Church and Anglican Communion joined together at the beginning of 2020 in a "Churchwide Bible Reading Initiative." https://www.episcopalchurch.org/publicaffairs/churchwide-bible -reading-initiative-continues-during-epiphany-2020/.

19 Not incidentally, sanctuary art in the form of triptychs and stained-glass windows, for example, did the same.

20 The Large Catechism followed and, while it was written primarily for clergy to advance their education, it was also accessible by laypeople who wished to continue and deepen their study of the faith.

21 Timothy J. Wengert, *The Small Catechism, 1529* (Minneapolis: Fortress, 2017): 263. Wengert quotes from Luther's 1528 *Ten Sermons on the Catechism,* LW 51:136–37.

22 Haemig, "Laypeople," 25.

23 Haemig, "Reclaiming," 43.

24 Haemig, 44–45. She goes on to write, "Learning the catechism became a way that laypersons were empowered to do what previously only a spiritual elite, members of an ecclesiastical hierarchy, had done: to judge what is true and false teaching. Learning the catechism gave ordinary people the function of oversight. This upended the hierarchy, in theory if not in practice" (45–46).

25 Haemig, 45.

26 Haemig, 47–48. She presses, "Paradoxically, at the same time that [Luther] empowered, he also subverted. That is, he subverted any claim that clergy might have the sole authority over reflection on the

faith. Do we see pastors today as empowering people and even sub-
verting their own claims? In what ways are laypeople today actively
holding pastors (or any authority, inside or outside the church)
accountable?"

27 Rose, *Sharing the Word*, 3.

28 Rebecca S. Chopp, *The Power to Speak: Feminism, Language, God* (New
York: Crossroad, 1989), 92, 95.

29 Rudolf Bohren, *Preaching and Community* (Richmond, VA: John
Knox, 1965), 132, quoted in Rose, *Sharing the Word*, 52.

30 Bohren, *Preaching and Community*, 128, in Rose, *Sharing the Word*, 52.

31 Rose, *Sharing the Word*, 52.

32 Hans Van Der Geest, *Presence in the Pulpit: The Impact of Personality
in Preaching*, trans. Douglass W. Stott (Louisville: John Knox, 1981),
31–68, quoted in Allen, "Turn to the Listener," 191.

33 Allen, "Turn to the Listener," 5.

34 Rose, *Sharing the Word*, 129.

35 Because rating preachers' sermons might trigger an adverse reaction
in preachers, when such feedback is desired (indeed, there is a time
and place for this kind of feedback), be sure to gather a group of
trusted people to provide support and care. In the summary of the
broad qualitative study "Listening to Listeners," the director, Ronald Allen, remarks, "In the early stages of the study, when we were
recruiting congregations to participate, our strategy was to approach
the minister with the initial invitation. Many preachers immediately
said, 'No thanks' to the possibility of participating in the preaching.
Some of those who said, 'No thanks' also said, in essence, 'I am not
ready to face what might come out.' The vulnerability required of the
clergy was too much for some. We wonder about the extent of this fac-
tor in influencing decisions not to participate in the project." From
footnote 10 of Allen, "Listening to Listeners," summary.

36 For a more focused reflection on the preacher as preacher, I recommend occasionally posing a different set of questions. Consider the
work of Stephen Brookfield, who suggests the following four questions: When were you most engaged? When were you least engaged?

What surprised you? What confused you? Brookfield, *Becoming a Critically Reflective Teacher*, 2nd ed. (San Francisco: Jossey-Bass, 2017).

37 Tom Long encourages preachers to identify a function statement for each sermon—that is, to identify what they hope will happen to those in the pews as a result of hearing the sermon. Long, *Witness of Preaching*, 127.

38 Allen, "Turn to the Listener," 167–96.

39 John McClure recommends combining the feedback from the previous sermon and the feedforward for the upcoming sermon. For a very helpful outline of McClure's recommendation, see McClure, "Collaborative Brainstorming: A Word to Preachers," in McClure, *Roundtable Pulpit*, 59–72.

40 Haemig, "Reclaiming," 45–46.

Chapter 7

1 See note 30 in chapter 5 (p. 213).

2 As an aside, I'm often invited to be a guest preacher in congregations. I am honored by and appreciate such invitations. But these days I ask if there isn't perhaps someone in the congregation who can preach while the preacher is on vacation. If not, I hope that my presence as the kind of guest preacher who requires engaging the feedforward and feedback process can be the start of encouraging congregational preachers to empower and equip other people in the congregation to preach.

3 A simple internet search will yield numerous uses and examples.

4 Rose, *Sharing the Word*, 131.

Appendix C

1 Thank you to Pastor Brenda Greenwald for the final three feedback forms.

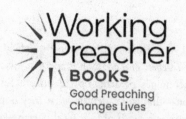

Books in the Series